THE LOGICAL MIND

THE LOGICAL MIND

*Learn Critical Thinking
To Make Better Choices*

M.A. APONTE

The Intellectual Library

Contents

CASE STUDIES

PART TEN
CONCLUSION AND NEXT STEPS

ISBN-13: 979-8-9885861-0-4

Cover design by: The Intellectual Library
Library of Congress Control Number: 2018675309
Printed in the United States of America

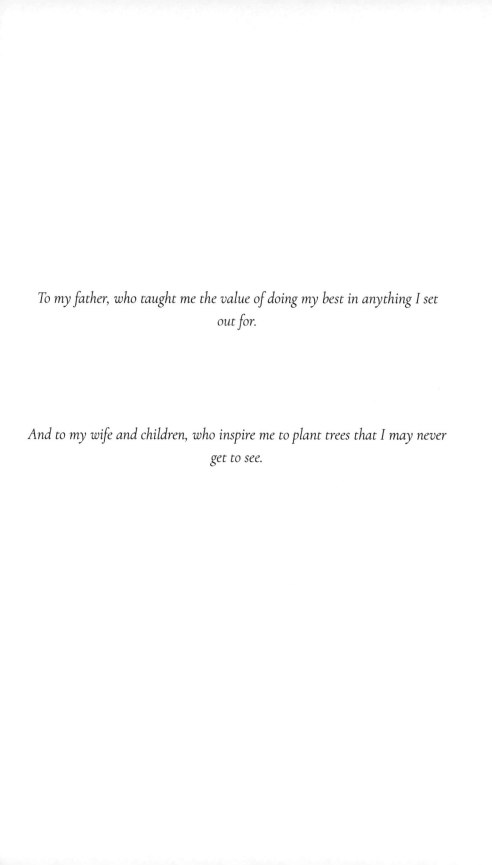

To my father, who taught me the value of doing my best in anything I set out for.

And to my wife and children, who inspire me to plant trees that I may never get to see.

PART ONE

Understanding Critical Thinking

I

⚜

Chapter 1: The Power of Critical Thinking

"A lie doesn't become truth, wrong doesn't become right, and evil doesn't become good, just because it's accepted by a majority"

—BOOKER T. WASHINGTON

In the modern world, we are continuously inundated with information coming from a wide range of sources, and it can be difficult to differentiate between sources that can be trusted and those that cannot be trusted. Critical thinking enables one to assess information in a manner that is both methodical and objective, which then enables one to make judgments that are more well-informed, successfully solve issues, and communicate more clearly. Critical thinking may also help you avoid being affected by biases and emotions, both of which can result in bad decision-making. In addition, it may assist you in your personal life by encouraging you to challenge assumptions and ideas that you might have had for a long time and to reevaluate whether or not they still hold true. This can be helpful in determining whether or not they are still relevant to your life.

The ability to think rationally, objectively, and logically about a topic or problem is one of the primary benefits of developing one's critical thinking skills. The act of examining and evaluating information, arguments, and assertions in order to come to rational conclusions and choices is known as critical thinking. In today's fast-paced climate, it might be tempting to make hasty judgments based on inadequate information, or to take information at face value without examining its veracity. Both of these practices should be avoided at all costs. But, the capacity to think critically is a crucial talent that may help you negotiate the intricacies of both your personal and professional life. This is true whether you are a young adult, a parent, or a professional. The purpose of this chapter is to present a definition of critical thinking, an explanation of its significance, and some instances of how it may be applied in a variety of settings.

The Value of Engaging in Reflective Thinking

Thinking critically entails using a methodical, organized approach to tasks such as analyzing data and coming to conclusions. It entails calling into question presumptions, taking facts into consideration, and analyzing the benefits and drawbacks of various solutions. When we are able to think critically, we are in a better position to make judgments that are both informed and accurate. This is true regardless of whether we are determining the best way to proceed with a work assignment or determining the dependability of a news source.

Additionally, the ability to think critically has far-reaching effects on our daily lives. If we strengthen our critical thinking skills, we may become better at problem solving, more effective communicators, and more resilient in the face of challenges and obstacles.

Suppose that you are at a shopping center and that you come across an advertisement for a new product that claims to be able to cure all of your skin issues. In addition to before-and-after photographs, client endorsements, and a promise to refund any money spent, the advertisement also includes a money-back guarantee. On the surface, it can appear like the product is an excellent remedy for the problems you're having with your skin. If you apply critical thinking, on the other hand, you could doubt the veracity of the testimonials and conduct some research to see whether or not there are any evaluations of the product written by independent parties. You should give some thought to the possible negatives of utilizing the product as well, such as any side effects or bad reactions that may occur. You will be in a better position to determine whether or not the item is suitable for you if you take an analytical approach and think things through.

The Art of Critical Thinking and Decision-Making

Both decision making and critical thinking are inextricably linked together. In order to make the best judgments possible, we need to be able to analyze information critically, take into account all of the important elements, and assess the benefits and drawbacks of the many choices available to us. When we approach decision making with a critical attitude, we are less likely to fall prey to cognitive biases and more inclined to make well-informed judgments that lead to good results. This is because cognitive biases are more likely to be triggered when we are under pressure.

Examples of Critical Thinking in Action

In order to better emphasize the significance of critical thinking, let's have a look at a few instances from real life:

Say you are in the market for a new automobile and have two brands to choose from: one is an established, dependable brand with a good name, and the other is a younger, more forward-thinking brand that offers the most up-to-date technology and amenities. Which one would you choose? In order to make an educated decision, you need to do an objective analysis of the benefits and drawbacks of each alternative, as well as a cost-benefit analysis of each potential course of action.

Let's have a look at some real-world applications of this skill so that we may better understand its significance:

- Choosing between two car options: You have the option of purchasing either a well-known and reputable brand that is renowned for its dependability, or a newer brand with the most recent technology and features. You will be able to make an informed decision that takes into account the potential risks and benefits of each option if you conduct a thorough analysis of both of these factors.
- Evaluating the Authenticity of Health Information: You come across an article claiming that a particular food could cause cancer. In order to determine whether or not this assertion is accurate, it is essential to conduct a thorough analysis of both the facts and the source of the information. Thus, you will be able to make an informed decision about whether or not to believe the information, and you can adjust your diet accordingly.

You will be able to make an informed decision about whether or not to believe the article and alter your diet in accordance with that decision if you think critically.

So what is critical thinking?

Critical thinking refers to the capacity to evaluate information, arguments, and assertions in order to reach well-informed conclusions. It necessitates analyzing the evidence, identifying any existing biases, and taking into account various points of view. In other words, it is the process of actively and objectively evaluating information to reach a conclusion that is well-supported by the evidence. In addition, the ability to question preconceived notions and distinguish between reliable and unreliable sources is crucial.

Difference between Critical Thinking and Other Forms of Thinking:

Critical thinking differs from other types of thought, such as creative and intuitive thinking. The process of developing fresh and distinctive ideas is known as creative thinking, whereas intuitive thinking is the process of making decisions based on gut feelings or intuition. The act of examining information, arguments, and claims in order to make sound conclusions and decisions, on the other hand, is known as critical thinking.

Common Misconceptions about Critical Thinking:

A common misconception about critical thinking is that it is only applicable in academic or professional settings. It is a valuable skill that can be utilized in many aspects of life, such as making independent decisions and accessing information online. Furthermore, some individuals conflate critical thinking with negativity or cynicism, but critical thinking is about being open-minded and evaluating claims based on evidence.

Examples of critical thinking in action

1. Problem-solving: Suppose you are working on a group project and one of your teammates is struggling to complete their assigned task. Instead of becoming frustrated, you analyze the situation and devise a solution using critical thinking. You could consider

alternative approaches, assess the advantages and disadvantages of each alternative, and then choose the optimal course of action.

2. Decision-making: Consider that your company is contemplating a substantial investment in a new product. As a manager, you evaluate the potential risks and benefits of the investment using critical thinking. Before making a decision, you might collect data, consider various scenarios, and weigh the costs and benefits.

3. Evaluating information: Suppose you're reading an online article about a new health supplement that makes a bold claim. Instead of accepting the claim without question, you evaluate the evidence presented in the article using critical thinking. Consider the information's source, search for other sources that confirm or refute the claim, and assess the evidence's credibility.

The Steps of the Critical Thinking Process:

The critical thinking process is divided into multiple parts, which include observation, analysis, interpretation, evaluation, and inference. These processes are vital to the critical thinking process and to assisting individuals in making accurate judgments and conclusions.

1. Observation: This is the first step in the process of critical thinking. Information is gathered through observation, research, and investigation. It is essential to pay close attention to the particulars and consider things from various perspectives.

2. Analysis: After collecting data, the next step is to analyze it by dissecting it into its component parts and examining them closely. This is where critical thinking comes into play, as it is necessary to ask questions, search for patterns, and determine how things are connected.

3. Interpretation: After examining the information and figuring

out what it means, the next step is to interpret it. Here, you need to be able to use your critical thinking skills to make sense of the information and understand how it was presented.

4. Evaluation: The following step is to evaluate the evidence, claims, and arguments. Here, critical thinking is used to evaluate the evidence and reasoning given and decide if it is valid, reliable, and convincing.

5. Inference: The process of critical thinking concludes with the step of drawing inferences from the facts, arguments, and statements that have been analyzed in the previous steps. For the purpose of arriving at logical conclusions and settling on courses of action, critical thinking skills are utilized here.

Examples of Applying Critical Thinking:

The ability to think critically can be put to use in a broad variety of contexts, including the analysis of information, the formulation of solutions to problems, and the selection of appropriate courses of action. The following are some examples:

- Problem-solving: A critical thinker would use the steps of the critical thinking process to gather information, analyze it, interpret it, evaluate it, and make an inference in order to come up with a solution when presented with a challenging situation.
- Making decisions: A critical thinker would utilize the steps of the critical thinking process to gather information, analyze it, interpret it, evaluate it, and make an inference to identify the best course of action to take while making an important decision.
- Information evaluation: Evaluating information requires a critical thinker to use the steps of the critical thinking process, which include gathering information, analyzing the information, interpreting the information, evaluating the information, and

drawing an inference from the information in order to determine whether or not the information is accurate and reliable.

Real world example:

1. Observation: When trying to figure out what's wrong with a car, a critical thinker would use the observation step to learn more about the car's symptoms. For instance, they might notice that the car starts up with a strange sound or that the engine light is on. They would also find out how well the car has been taken care of and if it has been fixed before. By collecting this information, a critical thinker can get a better grasp of the problem and move on to the next step.

2. Analysis: After getting information, the next step is to figure out what it all means. For instance, a critical thinker might look at the signs that something is wrong with the car and compare them to a list of common car problems. They might also look at the history of repairs and maintenance to see if there are any patterns or links. By analyzing the information, a critical thinker can narrow down the possible causes of the problem and move on to the next step.

3. Interpretation: After analyzing the information, the next step is to figure out what it means. For example, a critical thinker might see the car's problems as signs that there might be a problem with the engine. They might also think that the car's maintenance record shows that it has been well taken care of. By figuring out how to interpret the information, a critical thinker can make sense of it and understand why it was given in the way it was.

4. Evaluation: The next step is to evaluate the arguments, claims, and information. For example, a critical thinker might think about how likely each of the possible reasons for the car problem is. They might also look at the history of repairs and maintenance

by looking at how well the work was done. By evaluating the information, a critical thinker can figure out if the evidence and reasoning given are valid, reliable, and convincing. In this case, a critical thinker would probably do research and check the information about what could be wrong with the car based on the symptoms and maintenance history, using the most accurate and reliable information to make a decision.

5. Inference: The last step in the critical thinking process is to draw conclusions from the evaluated facts, arguments, and claims. A critical thinker might, for example, figure out that the problem with the car is caused by a broken part in the engine and that it will need to be replaced. They might also think that taking the car to a mechanic for a proper diagnosis and repair is the best thing to do. By making inferences, a critical thinker can come to logical conclusions and make decisions based on the evidence and reasoning given.

These examples illustrate how the steps of the critical thinking process can be implemented in real-world scenarios and how the steps are interconnected with one another. Inference and decision making are the end results of observation, analysis, interpretation, and evaluation. Each of these steps must be carried out with a certain degree of objectivity and impartiality, and one must be willing to consider all of the evidence, even if it runs counter to one's preconceptions or biases. More will be spoken about this at a later time.

The ability to think critically is an essential skill that enables us to make well-informed decisions, find solutions to difficult issues, and get a better understanding of the world around us. It is a skill that can be learned and refined over time, and it's a crucial tool for navigating the intricacies of the modern world. By increasing our critical thinking skills, we can become better problem solvers, more effective communicators, and more resilient in the face of challenges and hurdles. And by addressing the process of decision making with a critical mindset, we may ensure that our decisions are well-informed and based on reliable information by approaching the decision making process with a critical perspective. In the following chapters, we will go deeper into the process of critical thinking and give you concrete ways for enhancing and putting this ability to use in both your personal and professional lives.

Ultimately, throughout this book you will find a number of case studies. These case studies provide samples of my own line of reasoning and arguments regarding various subjects. I am providing you with these essays so that you can get a sense of how to guide your mind through the confusing maze of knowledge, or lack of information. In addition, the majority of difficult concepts, if not all of them, should be explored, thought through, and written down in order to get a deeper level of comprehension. You do not need to have excellent writing skills (such as grammar, spelling, or punctuation), but you do need to be able to organize your thoughts, and there is no other discipline that can help you accomplish that as well as writing. This might take the shape of a diary or journal. This book is intended for you to write in it, respond to questions, engage in self-reflection, and get the creative writing process started. I can teach you critical thinking, but you need to execute your part for the lessons to be effective.

Questions

1. What is your current understanding of critical thinking?
2. How do you currently approach decision making and evaluating information?
3. Can you identify a situation where you could have used critical thinking skills to make a better decision?
4. How do you plan to improve your critical thinking skills in the future?
5. How do you see critical thinking impacting your personal or professional life?
6. What steps can you take to develop your critical thinking skills?
7. Can you think of any real-life examples where critical thinking would be useful?

II

⚬⚬

Chapter 2: What Critical Thinking is Not

"Knowledge is not made for understanding; it is made for cutting."

—MICHEL FOUCAULT

Critical thinking and critical theory - two seemingly similar terms but with distinct differences. Critical theory is a progressive theory that dives deeper into the investigation of power structures and societal norms, as well as the influence these have on individuals and groups, whereas critical thinking focuses on the development of human thought and reasoning.

It is possible to trace the origins of critical thinking all the way back to Socrates in the 5th century BC. Afterwards, philosopher John Dewey promoted the concept of critical thinking as an essential component of a democratic society. According to Dewey, a society that places a high priority on critical thinking will naturally develop a higher level of knowledge and education. In contrast, critical theory, which centers on social criticism, was established in the 20th century by numerous intellectuals as a tool to challenge dominant power systems. Its primary focus is on social critique.

So, what are the characteristics of a person who is able to think critically? It's the ability to analyze facts to form a logical judgment and requires the development of self-directed, self-disciplined, self-monitored, and self-corrective thinking. A person who questions, investigates, hypothesizes, experiments, observes, draws conclusions, and shares their results is said to have critical thinking skills. They are aware of the significance of logic in reasoning and employ several types of logical reasoning, including deductive, abductive, and inductive reasoning. A critical thinker is a logical minded individual.

Logic is a part of both mathematics and philosophy. It is the study of reasoning, arguments, and the conditions under which an inference can be considered valid. It is a systematic way to judge the validity of arguments, draw conclusions, and draw inferences. Logic can be used in many ways, but the most common are the inductive, abductive, and deductive ways of thinking. Please keep in mind that you don't have to know how to solve every logical equation, but you should know what the different kinds are.

Deductive reasoning starts with a general statement or principle and then applies it to a specific situation to come to a logical conclusion. The conclusion must logically follow from the premises, and if the premises are true, then the conclusion must also be true. Most people agree that this kind of logic is the most sure and reliable. Example: "All men are mortal. Socrates was a person who was a man. Socrates is a mortal being because of this."

Inductive reasoning, on the other hand, is when you draw conclusions based on patterns or generalizations you see in specific observations or events. Using specific examples is one way to do this. When you use inductive reasoning, you can come to a conclusion that has a high chance of being right, but you can't be sure because it's based on evidence instead of being deductively certain. Example: "I've never seen a bird when it wasn't flying. Because of this, every bird is able to fly." Without being aware that not all birds can fly.

Abductive reasoning, which is also called "inference to the best explanation," starts with an observation and tries to find the simplest and most likely explanation for that observation. Inference to the best explanation is another name for this type of reasoning. Using abductive reasoning to come to a conclusion is not a sure thing, but it is the most likely explanation based on the facts and information that are now known. Example: "The lights in the sky are going in different directions and moving around. The most likely idea is that it is some kind of flying saucer."

There are many distinct types of logic, each of which has its own rules and procedures for constructing arguments:

Propositional logic is the study of the logical operations that can be done on propositions, which are statements that can be true or false. It is also called sentential logic or propositional calculus. Logic connectives like "and," "or," "not," "if-then," and "if and only if" are used to make complex statements in this way of thinking. These links are used to figure out if an argument makes sense or not. For example, the statement "A and B" is true if both "A" and "B" are true. However, the statement "A or B" is true if either "A" or "B" is true.

Predicate logic, which is also called first-order logic, makes it possible to show how different things relate to each other. This is an extension of propositional logic. In this type of logic, statements about objects and their relationships are made using predicates, which are functions that turn the state of an item into a truth value, and quantifiers, which are operators that show how many objects a predicate applies to. For example, "Every human being has a limited amount of time to live" can be written as "Human(x) is equal to Mortal(x)" in predicate logic. To elaborate on this example, if we want to say that all humans are mortal, we can use the predicate "Mortal(x)" to indicate that the property of being mortal applies to any object x that is described as human. This statement can be written as "For all x, if x is human, then x is mortal," using the universal quantifier "for all x."

Modal logic is a type of logic that looks at things like what is viable, what is necessary, and what is possible. Modal logics are used to formalize reasoning about many kinds of possibility and necessity, like physical necessity, logical necessity, and epistemic possibility. Modal logics are also used to codify arguments about logical contradictions. For example, the statement "All bachelors must be single" could be written as "Bachelor(x) Unmarried(x)," where x is the variable to be compared. Modal logic is also useful for dealing with logical inconsistencies, and for capturing the reasoning involved in resolving them. By formalizing statements about different kinds of necessity and possibility, modal logic allows us to reason about complex systems and to make precise statements about the relationships between different propositions.

Deontic logic is a type of modal logic that tries to figure out how to put moral and legal rules into words. Deontic logic gives us a way to think about the relationships between obligations, permissions, and bans. In the context of deontic logic, "Smoking is not allowed in this building" can be written as "Smoking(x) -Permitted(x)," where the minus sign means that something is not allowed. This sentence means that smoking is not allowed in the building for any object x that is described as smoking. In fields like ethics, law, and social and political philosophy, deontic logic is used to formalize reasoning about moral and legal rules and to figure out how different kinds of obligations, permissions, and bans relate to each other. Deontic logic can help clarify ethical and legal debates and solve conflicts between different moral and legal rules by giving us a formal way to think about how these relationships work.

The formalization of reasoning in relation to time is the focus of the branch of logic known as temporal logic, which is a subset of modal logic. Temporal logic lets us think about how events happen, how long they last, and what order they take place in. For example, in temporal logic, the statement "If John turns off the lights, it will be dark" can be written as "TurnOffLights(John) Dark(x)," where TurnOffLights stands for John turning off the lights and Dark stands for the room getting dark. This sentence means, "It will be dark if John turns off the lights." Temporal logic is used in many fields, like computer science, artificial intelligence, and philosophy, to reason about the temporal properties of systems and events, check the correctness of programs and protocols, and study what time is. By giving us a formal way to think about time, temporal logic can help us understand and change how things happen at different times.

Relevance logic gives us a way to think about how ideas fit into the situation in which they are being thought about. For example, the statement "If it rains, you will need an umbrella" can be interpreted in relevance logic as "Rain(x) implies Umbrella(y)," which emphasizes the relationship between the event of rain and the action of needing an umbrella. In relevance logic, whether a statement is true or false depends on how it fits into the situation where it is being judged. This makes it easier to reason when the meaning of a statement is not clear or changes depending on the situation. Relevance logic helps us understand and reason about the relationships between ideas and how they apply to the situations in which they are being evaluated. It does this by focusing on how important a statement is in a certain situation.

These are some of the most common approaches of logical thinking. Each type of logic has its own rules and ways to make arguments, and each is best for different kinds of reasoning and uses. Since each kind of logic has a unique set of advantages and disadvantages, these types of logic are often combined in order to get a more thorough and accurate understanding of any particular scenario or challenge. One may get a more in-depth grasp of reasoning, arguments, and the standards for making valid inferences by studying the many distinct types of logic.

In addition, critical thinking requires separating one's emotions from the decision-making process and placing one's whole trust in the evidence presented. Critical thinkers frequently find refuge in the scientific method as a technique to approach ideas, issues, or situations. This is because critical thinking frequently involves practice and discipline. Finding solutions can also be accomplished by critical thinkers through the use of the research method, which is a methodical process for acquiring and evaluating observations.

Finally, I must stress again: Critical thinking and critical theory share the same prefix, but they are not the same thing at all; rather, they are two unique ways of approaching thought and problem-solving that have nothing in common. Critical thinking is an individual process that involves reasoning and decision-making, whereas critical theory is focused on analyzing society's power systems and criticizing social institutions. They are not equivalent in any way.

Questions

Deductive Reasoning:

1. What is the definition of deductive reasoning?
2. Give an example of a deductive argument in your own words.
3. Can you identify the premises and conclusion in the following argument: "All dogs are animals. Spot is a dog. Therefore, Spot is an animal."
4. Is the following argument deductive or inductive: "Most people in the city drive cars, therefore I will assume that the person I am meeting today also drives a car."

Inductive Reasoning:

1. What is the definition of inductive reasoning?
2. Give an example of an inductive argument in your own words.
3. Can you explain the difference between deductive and inductive reasoning?
4. Is the following argument deductive or inductive: "Every time I have taken a plane, it has arrived on time. Therefore, I can conclude that all planes always arrive on time."

Abductive Reasoning:

1. What is the definition of abductive reasoning?
2. Give an example of an abductive argument in your own words.
3. Can you explain the difference between deductive and abductive reasoning?
4. Is the following argument abductive or deductive: "The lights are on in the house and there is music playing. It must be a party."

General Logic:

1. Can you define logic?

2. What is the purpose of using logic in arguments and discussions?
3. Can you give an example of a logical fallacy and explain why it is fallacious?
4. Why is it important to understand the different forms of logic and how to distinguish between them?

III

⚭

Chapter 3: Take the emotions out of big decision making.

"It is the mark of an educated mind to be able to entertain a thought without accepting it."

—ARISTOTLE

Taking emotions out of the equation is often the probably the most difficult part of making a decision. Many times, the decisions we make are based on how we feel. These decisions can lead to wealth or poverty, life or death, lasting love or short-lived passion. Still, we need to use our critical thinking skills when we come to a fork in the road. Let's use the most simple and common example to explain this idea: If you could choose between broccoli and pizza, would you always choose broccoli? For me, the answer is an obvious no! Some things in life are hard to deny. But the overall conclusions and goals should be what most of your decisions are based on. You should always answer to yourself. Did you always pick Pizza? Do you know how your blood pressure and cholesterol levels are doing? For many Americans, heart disease is the silent killer. What will happen if I have "1 more slice"? And if you chose that extra piece, how many times have you made the same choice? The small decisions you make will add up to have big effects on your life in the long run. This is an example of a time when you need to decide if you should use your head or your heart. This is a Stoic philosophy.

Stoicism is a way of life that comes from ancient Greece. It is more than just a theory or piece of advice. Many religious and philosophical systems, such as Christianity, Judaism, Islam, Buddhism, and others, credit this philosophy with having an effect on their moral views. Even Buddhism and stoicism have a lot in common in a variety of ways. During the Roman Empire, Stoicism was seen as the right way to live, and many of its great leaders, like Marcus Aurelius, who was one of Rome's best emperors, followed it. But this isn't just a philosophical way of life and the basis for people who can think critically. Stoicism can also be found in popular books about leadership. It's all around us, but most people have never heard of it or have the wrong idea about it.

In many ways, the Stoics of old were the first people to teach us how to think critically. How else can you look at a situation, take your feelings out of it, look at all the different points of view and evidence, find any possible causes, and then come to a conclusion that you may or may not agree with? This is what Stoicism is all about. People who really wanted to understand it looked for its wisdom. This idea has also been used by many great leaders throughout history, such as George Washington, who is known as the father of the United States, Frederick the Great, who ruled the Kingdom of Prussia for the longest time, and Immanuel Kant, who was a famous German philosopher and one of the most influential Enlightenment thinkers.

Stoicism teaches its learners to make judgments and evaluate circumstances objectively, free from the influence of their emotions and irrational attachments to particular outcomes. This requires considering all of the information and points of view, locating those who were harmed, and arriving at a conclusion that may or may not be in line with our emotions. This is the essence of stoicism, and the reason why it has been practiced by enlightened individuals throughout the course of history.

Three examples show how Stoicism can be used in the real world. The first is Marcus Aurelius, who was born in 121 and died in 180. From 161 to 180, when he was emperor of Rome, he had to deal with a pandemic called the Antonine Plague. Most people wanted him to run away, but he didn't. Instead, he stayed with the people, going to funerals with them and talking to them. He thought that it was his job to be a citizen, not an emperor, and that his main goal should be to keep Rome alive. Even though he lost most of his money, possessions, and six of his children, he stayed calm and focused on the end goal. He set an example for how to make good decisions when your emotions are getting in the way.

The second example is Theodore Roosevelt, who was shot in the chest in 1912 while running for president of the United States. He refused to go to the hospital, though. Instead, he insisted on speaking to the crowd. He walked onto the stage and said, "I don't know if you fully understood that I had just been shot, but it will take more than that to kill a bull moose." This example shows how we can be our own limits and how every unexpected thing that happens in life is a chance to grow, as long as we accept, appreciate, and deal with it objectively instead of letting our feelings take over. Roosevelt also knew that this was a chance to show how things should be done, not a problem. Everything that goes wrong in your life is a chance to get better.

Jackie Robinson, a professional baseball player, is an example of someone who put aside his feelings not only to make good decisions but also as a way to get even (B. 1919- D. 1972). Before 1947, people of color could not play in major league baseball. But the Dodgers were the first team to sign a black man, which was a sign that segregation by race should end in the sport. Jackie Robinson and Branch Rickey, the president and general manager of the Dodgers, talked about it like this: "Do you have the guts?" Robinson answers, "Mr. Rickey, are you looking for a black person who won't fight back?" Rickey responds, "Robinson, I'm looking for a ball player with the guts to NOT fight back." These strong words made Jackie Robinson's legacy, not just in baseball but also in modern history and the civil rights movement. Robinson also knew that if he fought back, it would not only end his career, but also turn back the movement toward desegregation that was happening at the time. Even though he was traveling with the team, he still had to deal with Jim Crow laws and segregation. He was turned away from hotels and restaurants, and the fans of opposing teams yelled racial slurs at him. He was not only tested, but he also agreed to take a "friendly" photo with Ben Chapman, the manager of the Philadelphia Phillies, who yelled racial slurs the whole game a month earlier. This was done to save Chapman's career. Robinson wrote in his memoir that he was angry and that it was one of the hardest things he had to do. But he did it because he knew it was part of a bigger plan, the great experiment of ending segregation and giving everyone the same chances. He also knew that if he wanted to do what he loved, which was baseball, he had to put up with the rudeness of others. Robinson was the Rookie of the Year, an All-Star for six straight years, and the Most Valuable Player during his ten-year career. All of the teams in his sport retired his uniform number 42, and on "Jackie Robinson Day," every player on every team wears number 42.

These examples show that it's not easy to make decisions in life without letting your feelings get in the way, especially when those decisions are hard. However, it's important and rewarding to do so. So how do you start doing this? We need to learn more about Stoic philosophy to start the process of making decisions without letting emotions get in the way.

Stoicism's four virtues are wisdom, fairness, courage, and moderation. Many university professors and philosophers still study and talk about what this really means. But in the end, wisdom comes down to a deep study and understanding of common sense, calculation, wit, discretion, and resourcefulness. This means that to be wise, with a logical mind, you need to be able to think critically in different ways and know when to use each one. You also need to know when to speak and when to be quiet and listen. Just treatment, equality, humility, and honesty are all essential components of justice. This isn't just about how to keep yourself in order. It's also about how to work and act with other people, and how to treat both your friends and your enemies. Courage is a unique word that doesn't fit the way we use it today. Instead, it goes deeper into embracing and living an uncomfortable life. Stoicism tells you that you should have problems, but not necessarily with other people. When you make yourself uncomfortable, you start to value what you have. Then there is temperance, which means to act in a balanced way. This can be too much of anything, from feelings to material things. For example, if you feel ecstasy because of someone else, you need to spend some time alone and feel uncomfortable without that person. If you are rich, you should leave wealth and luxury for a few days. Furthermore, temperance, in essence means just because you can, doesn't mean you should.

Now that you know the four values, you can start to think about how to make a decision without letting your feelings get in the way. It might sound hard or even impossible, but you can do it if you try. Over time, this gets easier, but you have to take the first step. This could mean writing in a journal at the end of the day. Not only a summary of how your day went, but also an analysis of the decisions you made and why you made them. The book "Meditation" by Marcus Aurelius was a real journal that the late emperor wrote and had published. These writings were not meant for other people to read. They were more for him to think about and reflect on. You can also start writing down things you wanted to post on social media but didn't. Or maybe I should say, stop doing this. Write it down and tear up the paper. If this doesn't help, start working out to get rid of some of your feelings before you make a decision or say something you'll probably regret later. People often say that social media ruins personal lives and career opportunities. Do not post anything that relates to your current emotional state, even a positive one, you will only bring attention to yourself and most of the time, regardless of the intentions, would be negative.

The overall strategy of removing your emotions out of the decision making process is to combine the features of stoic philosophy and begin with the end goal in mind. Are your feelings right now getting in the way of your end goal? Chances are, if you have a goal, getting there will be hard. If you give in to these feelings, you will only delay or get rid of any chance of success. To be good at critical thinking, you need to have the Stoic virtues of wisdom, justice, courage, and moderation. This takes confidence, a strong will, and a lot of practice, because you are likely to fail a lot. That's fine! If everyone in society were stoic and a critical thinker, we wouldn't have half of the problems we do now. Henry Ford once said, "Whether you think you can or you think you can't, you're right." This is true when it comes to making decisions without letting your emotions get in the way.

Questions

1. What is the Stoicism philosophy and how has it influenced the lives of people in the past?
2. Why is it important to remove emotions from decision-making and analyze a situation objectively in the context of Stoicism?
3. Can you provide an example of Marcus Aurelius and how he applied Stoicism in the face of adversity?
4. How did Theodore Roosevelt demonstrate Stoicism in his life?
5. Can you discuss how Jackie Robinson applied Stoicism in his life and how it influenced the civil rights movement?

IV

❦

Chapter 4: The Science and Art of Critical Thinking

"I have never let my schooling interfere with my education."

—MARK TWAIN

Have you ever found yourself blindly accepting someone else's opinion without bothering to do your own research? In today's fast-paced, information-saturated world, it's more important than ever to be a critical thinker. But what exactly is critical thinking, and why is it so important? Let's first recap:

Reminder of The Definition of Critical Thinking

As discussed in chapter 1, Critical thinking is the systematic evaluation of information and arguments in order to make well-reasoned decisions and reach logical conclusions. It involves an open-minded, analytical approach to gathering and evaluating information, and the ability to recognize and overcome cognitive biases. In other words, the art of sifting through info and arguments, so you can make smart decisions and arrive at logical conclusions. It's all about taking a fair-minded, analytical approach to collecting and assessing information, and being able to recognize and combat any sneaky cognitive biases that might be lurking in your brain. In short, critical thinking is like a superpower that helps you cut through the noise and get to the heart of the matter.

Benefits of Critical Thinking

Critical thinking is a valuable tool for making informed decisions, as it allows you to gather and evaluate information from multiple sources, challenge your own beliefs, and come to your own conclusions. By developing your critical thinking skills, you'll become a more independent thinker, capable of making choices that align with your own beliefs and values. In other words, If you're looking to make better decisions and truly stand behind your choices, then critical thinking is your go-to tool. This approach enables you to gather insights and weigh up information from different sources, question your own assumptions, and arrive at well-thought-out conclusions. By honing your critical thinking skills, you'll not only become a savvy decision-maker but also a more autonomous thinker who can trust their instincts and align their actions to the most appropriate outcome.

Challenges of Critical Thinking

Despite its many benefits, being a critical thinker isn't always easy. It can be tough to challenge your own beliefs, listen to opposing viewpoints, and overcome cognitive biases. Common biases to watch out for include confirmation bias, the halo effect, and the sunk cost fallacy. However, like any skill, the more you practice, the better you'll get.

Strategies for Developing Critical Thinking Skills

So, how do you flex your critical thinking muscles? Start by asking yourself questions: Why do you believe what you believe? What evidence do you have to support your position? And what other perspectives are out there? Additionally, consider the following strategies:

1. Gather information from a variety of sources. For example, instead of just reading one news article about a topic, consider reading articles from multiple perspectives to get a more well-rounded understanding of the issue.
2. Challenge your own beliefs and assumptions. Ask yourself what evidence you have to support your position, and be open to the possibility that you may be wrong.
3. Practice active listening and engage in respectful dialogue with people who have different viewpoints. This will help you to understand their perspective and consider alternative viewpoints.
4. Be aware of your own cognitive biases and take steps to overcome them. For example, if you tend to believe things that confirm your existing beliefs, make a conscious effort to seek out information that contradicts those beliefs.
5. Continuously evaluate and refine your critical thinking skills. Regularly reflect on your decision-making processes and consider what you could have done differently to be a more critical thinker.

One of the key components of critical thinking is the ability to analyze information and arguments in a systematic and objective way. The critical thinking process is a structured approach to evaluating information and making well-supported conclusions. In this chapter, we will outline the steps of the critical thinking process, provide examples of how to apply them to different types of situations, and further elaborate on the purpose and goals of each step.

Step 1: Observation

In order to begin the process of critical thinking, the first step is observation. Collecting information and facts pertaining to the problem or issue at hand is a necessary step in this process. The goal of this stage is to amass as much pertinent information as is humanly possible while maintaining an objective stance and avoiding hasty conclusions based on information that is either insufficient or skewed in some way. Direct observation or research through secondary sources are both valid methods for accomplishing this goal. A detective who is looking into a crime scene, for instance, will examine the evidence, note the location, and make a mental note of any potential witnesses. In a similar manner, a mechanic who is diagnosing a problem with an automobile's engine will examine the vehicle itself, listen to the engine, and collect any other information that may be relevant to determining the source of the issue. The most important thing is to keep one's personal biases and assumptions out of the way so that one can concentrate on the facts, figures, and data that are pertinent to the problem or issue at hand.

Step 2: Analysis

Following the completion of the step in which you gather information, the next step is to analyze the data. This requires segmenting the information into smaller pieces, recognizing patterns and connections, and searching for any inconsistencies or contradictions that may exist. You will be able to acquire a more in-depth understanding of the information as well as identify any potential issues or areas of concern thanks to this step. This stage of the process should center on the search for the underlying causes, the identification of any patterns or trends, and the comprehension of how the information relates to the issue at hand. For example, if you're a manager looking at a new project proposal, you would analyze the data, identifying any trends or patterns that would indicate the project's feasibility or potential impact. Or, if you're an engineer trying to solve a technical problem, you would analyze the data and the design of the system to understand what might be causing the problem.

Step 3: Interpretation

The third step is known as interpretation, and it involves making sense of the information and attempting to comprehend the significance of what it means. In this stage, you will evaluate the information and determine how it relates to other information and how it can be applied to a variety of different settings. Making connections and gaining an understanding of the meaning of the information, as well as its implications and potential impact, should be the primary focuses of this step. For instance, if you are reading an article about a new health supplement, you would interpret the information by taking into consideration the source of the information, searching for other sources that either confirm or refute the claim, and evaluating the credibility of the evidence. Alternatively, if you are a scientist who is analyzing an experiment, you would interpret the results by determining what they mean in the context of your research question and how they relate to other experiments or studies. This would be done in order to draw any conclusions about the experiment.

Step 4: Evaluation

The fourth step is called "evaluation," and it entails making a decision about the value or significance of the information that was gathered. The next step is to examine the evidence, evaluate the credibility of the arguments, and determine the reliability of the sources used in the investigation. At this stage, the focus should be on determining the credibility and quality of the information as well as how it relates to the issue or decision that is currently being considered.

For instance, if you are a political analyst and you are evaluating a news article about a political campaign, you would evaluate the credibility of the sources and the quality of the arguments presented in order to determine whether or not the claims that are made in the article are credible or not. Or, if you are a physician looking into new treatment options for a disease, you would look at the evidence that has been gathered from studies to determine which treatment options are both safe and effective.

Step 5: Inference

Inference is the last step in the process, and it consists of drawing a conclusion or making a prediction based on the information and analysis that was previously presented. In order to complete this step, you will need to apply your analytical thinking skills in order to determine the optimal next step or the result that is most likely to occur. At this stage, the focus should be on drawing logical conclusions and making predictions based on the information and analysis that was previously gathered. For instance, if you were a detective investigating a crime, you would use inference to draw conclusions about the guilt or innocence of a suspect based on the evidence collected. Similarly, if you were a business analyst, you would use inference to predict how a potential change in the market would affect the company's revenue. Both of these examples involve drawing conclusions about the suspect's actions based on the evidence collected.

Examples of the critical thinking process in action

1. Problem-solving: As a young adult, you might find yourself having a difficult conversation with a friend or a family member, with the disagreement arising from different perspectives and misunderstandings. In this case, you can use the critical thinking process to analyze the situation by observing the conversation and the body language of the other person, interpret the underlying reasons for the disagreement, evaluate different options for responding, and infer the best way to proceed.

2. Decision-making: As a professional, let's say you're a business analyst and your company is considering a merger with another company. You can use the critical thinking process to evaluate

the potential risks and benefits of the merger by observing and analyzing the financial data of both companies, interpreting the implications of the merger, evaluating the credibility of the sources and the viability of the plans and finally make inferences on whether the merger would be beneficial or not.

3. Evaluating information: As a young adult, you're researching different colleges and universities. You can use the critical thinking process to evaluate the information by observing and analyzing the statistics and the ranking of the schools, interpreting the data in relation to your own needs and preferences, evaluating the credibility of the sources, and making inferences about which schools would be the best fit for you.

4. Critical thinking and problem solving in healthcare: You're a nurse in a hospital, a patient complains of stomach pain. You observe the patient, gather information about their history and symptoms, analyze the information, interpret what could be causing the pain, evaluate the treatment options, infer the most appropriate course of action.

By following the critical thinking process, you can approach information and arguments in a systematic and objective way, which can help you to make more informed decisions, solve problems more effectively, and communicate more clearly. In the next chapters we will focus on specific aspects of critical thinking such as identifying and evaluating arguments, overcoming cognitive biases and applying critical thinking in different areas of life.

Cognitive biases are the unconscious mental shortcuts that can lead us to make inaccurate or irrational decisions. Understanding these biases is an essential part of developing critical thinking skills. One of the most common cognitive biases is confirmation bias, where individuals seek out information that supports their preconceived notions and ignore information that contradicts them. Another example is the sunk cost fallacy, where individuals make decisions based on the amount of resources already invested in a project, rather than on its potential return.

By being aware of these biases, individuals can take steps to avoid them, and make more informed decisions. This may involve seeking out information from a variety of sources, considering multiple perspectives, and engaging in ongoing self-reflection to check for biases in thinking.

Critical thinking is an essential tool for making informed decisions. By developing your critical thinking skills, you'll become a more independent thinker, capable of making choices that align with your own beliefs and values. So, the next time you're faced with a difficult decision, ask yourself: Am I being a critical thinker? And if not, what steps can I take to improve? With practice and dedication, you'll become a critical thinking superstar in no time!

Questions

1. Recap: What is critical thinking and why is it important? How does it compare to other forms of thinking?
2. How do you apply the steps of critical thinking in a real-life scenario? Evaluate a recent decision you made and explain how you could have applied critical thinking to it.
3. What are the advantages and disadvantages of being a critical thinker? How do you balance being open-minded with maintaining your own beliefs and values?
4. How do you identify and overcome cognitive biases in your decision-making process? Provide examples of biases you have experienced and explain how you addressed them.
5. How do you continuously assess and improve your critical thinking skills? Design a plan for regular self-reflection and explain how it will help you to grow as a critical thinker.

PART TWO

The Critical Thinking
Process

V

Chapter 5: Deconstruct your plans; beyond the "SMART goal" strategy

"A journey of a thousand miles must begin with a single step."

—LAO TZU

An important skill that all critical thinkers have is the ability to create a plan that is creative and sound. If you simply apply an action to get to a goal is not enough. If the action is not relevant to the plan, then you are simply being busy. However, if your action is relevant and measured, it is productive. People can spend hours in a meeting or classroom being busy and performing useless tasks but that doesn't mean they are not busy. They are simply being active. But if that meeting or classroom has an actual objective and all tasks are relevant, it can be almost inspiring because you are one step closer to an objective. Unfortunately, and fortunately depending on your perspective, it takes more than simply acting on relevance. Critical thinkers must always think of the "big picture" with the end goal in mind. But what if your end goal seems nearly impossible? What if you're a teenager who has inspiration to be an astronaut or a professional athlete? Can you quantify, or measure, a goal and figure out how to reach. The answer, in my humblest opinion, is yes! First, let's examine the life of someone who had several careers that all have a significant high level of entry. I want to analyze my life.

Case Study Before We Dive Deeper to SMART goals

Although there is a chapter focused on case studies to give you examples of critical thinking with different topics, this case study helps you understand the ideas of looking beyond the "SMART" goals: I was raised in public housing in Queens, New York. My father was an Emergency Medical Technician with a high school diploma. My mother, on the other hand, was an immigrant from Colombia, with a 3rd grade education, couldn't read in her own native language (Spanish), and she worked as a housekeeper in a hotel. I dropped out in the 10th grade in which it significantly lowered my chances in life for success. I earned my GED through 8 hours of studying, 7 days a week. I didn't like doing it but I kept reminding myself this is not forever and the big picture was my degree. This was the first real success in my life and the first time I ever experienced working with the end goal in mind. The feeling was unimaginable. I hated the restrictions I gave myself but felt an overwhelming sensation of euphoria when I received my results a week before my 18th birthday and several weeks before my high school graduating class of 2000. Nevertheless, I knew I had to earn this feeling again and began my next goal, be a commander of a combat unit. This would require going to college, something I never knew anyone doing within my inner circle of influence. However, the internet wasn't the main platform of information at the time so while working, I visited the library and began reading about college, military, and successful people's life. After much struggle, mistakes, and immature decisions, I reached the end goal and was assigned to the Combat Engineers branch in the Army, I completed my Officer's training. However, this was short lived and I was dismissed for "lack of motivation", which was not far from the truth since the war in Iraq took the life of my brother-in-law, Sgt. Angelo Lozada who I loved as if he was my blood brother, and I was living with someone at the time who was giving me the ultimatum, the Army or her. Ironically, the only time I decided to not follow my end goal would be the only time that I will have the biggest regret in my life. No other memory supersedes this one and it is this memory that has become my clutch when the end goal seems to fade.

With no prospects of a career, I decided to make a plan and pursue a life in wall street. I have met several stock brokers during my time in college and their success inspired me. So I used my experience working in retail and my training in the army to show discipline, updated my resume, and apply to every trainee job I can find. At the time, stock broker trainees were given a stipend instead of an actual salary or pay and this ranged around $300 a week. You also were not allowed to receive commission because it was illegal unless you have your broker license. Nevertheless, knowing these parameters, I was accepted as a trainee with a company located across the street from what was ground zero of the World Trade Center (a constant reminder to what I wanted to do when I was a teenager, be a commander in a special forces unit hunting down terrorists). I also lived with a woman who I didn't expect to provide for me while I learned my new trade, so I took up a night job at a retail store (overstocking). Sleeping was a luxury that could not be afforded. Eventually, after studying and working ridiculous amounts of hours per week that would be considered borderline indentured servitude, I did earn my Series 7 license. However, the company was being investigated on allegations I never knew about (they rarely spoke to the "rookies") and my Series 7 broker license can provide me a job that will pay me better, so I left the company to be a banker. This wasn't the end goal and it was actually a longer detour but it was still relevant to the goals I had. Eventually my success and hard work as a banker gave me an opportunity to be head hunted, recruiters who were courting me to go work for other companies and, if hired, would get paid up front! I eventually moved to Merrill Lynch as a wealth manager. I reached my end goal but I was already making plans for a new goal.

During the mortgage crisis between 2007-2009, which was known as the "great recession", I was working at Merrill Lynch. I reached my goal but the timing of this crisis came at the worst possible time. I was new and finally started to have a comfortable living. But the writing was all over the wall, the company that survived the great depression of 1929-1933, couldn't survive this economic crisis. I decided to create my own consulting company and while building that company, work for a pharmaceutical company as a representative. It was the most financially rewarding move I have done. However, this didn't last and eventually the economy caught up to me. I was laid off and, almost simultaneous, regulatory fees and insurance went up in the financial sector. I couldn't afford running my company. Being unemployed again and breaking up with the person who "inspired" me to sabotage my career in the Army, I had to do a major reset in my life. I wanted to focus on passions rather than wealth. One interest I always had was acting and the performing arts. Now, with the internet in full bloom, I researched online, read books on the craft and the market of acting (yes, acting is not just an art but you need to understand the market!), and applied to acting schools that offered free or reduced cost tuition.

With the focus with the "end goal in mind" to one day perform on television and stage in front of an audience. I eventually became a student and member in schools/groups such as, The Puerto Rican Traveling Theater, HB Studio and Stella Adler Studio of Acting. These prestigious organizations created well known actors you see in your favorite streaming services and movie theaters. They created the outlet I needed at the time. The friends I made along the way were different from the ones I made back in Wall Street or my old neighborhood projects prior to that. They gave me new, and unique, perspectives in how the world was viewed. Nevertheless, the feeling of wanting to do something more began to creep back into my conscious self. I began to study and train to be a police officer. In New York City, after you pass the test, the process can take up to three years just to get a phone call for a background check. The information that is gathered alone is enough to convince people that law enforcement may not be for them. I cannot speak for anyone outside of the United States, due to my lack of knowledge, but culturally Americans love to keep private matters outside of government meddling. Nevertheless, the process to be a police officer is the most intrusive process that any American can go through outside of obtaining a "Top Secret" clearance within the government. I am confident, if politicians, who create policies and laws that police officers have to enforce, had the same background checks, we would have entirely different elected members across the board. But I digress. The level of entry just before reaching the doors to the academy is difficult, not impossible. Eventually, I went through the academy with ease thanks to my prior training (also, considered an "old man" in my class) and became a police officer. However, It was my experience in the police department that showed me my true calling.

The amount of criminals I arrested for bad decision making, lack of opportunity, and lack of knowledge was so high that when I moved to Florida to be closer to my sick father, I decided to pursue a career in teaching. This required me to go back to school and earn my certification in teaching. That means, I had to humble myself (again), now in my mid-30's to sit and work with younger students and take undergraduate courses on being a teacher. My original plan was to attend graduate school and be a policy maker to help fix our educational system so that we can have a more productive society but I needed to be a teacher first and that made sense. How can I help teachers solve the problems if I do not know what they go through? How can I earn their respect if I do not understand them? This is my long term goal now and still working on as of this writing.

My experience alone can probably be a book on its own, and I believe so can yours. But what you just read was an excerpt that excluded many of the trials and tears that I had to go through in order to reach my goals. Each goal required me to be specific on what I needed to do to get into those careers, measure my progress to see if I am on the right track, complete realistic actions consistently, and keep track of the time it took for me to complete my goals. My life literally depended on it. But now it is time to focus on yours. How did someone from the housing projects of New York City, who was a highschool dropout, create opportunities for himself while others who he knew closely fell into drugs, prison, or death? You first need to think of a goal you want, not a dream. If you are standing at 4 foot 11, regardless of how much you train, the chances of you becoming the next basketball player is somewhere between slim to none. Sorry, we play with the cards we have been dealt in life. However, fortunately for you, most careers and aspirations can be planned! It is a matter of proper planning, focus, and a hunger to want it is the key.

Basic Introduction to SMART Goals

Let us begin with planning, out of all the studies and research that is out there, the one that can hold true is the S.M.A.R.T goal. The creation of the strategy was originally in 1968 by Dr. Edwin Locke, who published a paper called the "Toward a Theory of Task Motivation and Incentives"[1]. But it was George T. Doran who coined the term "SMART" planning[2]. These ideas were originally created for organizations and companies but can, and should, be applied to your life. The acronym and principles of the "SMART" goals are:

- Specific: A specific item or target improvement/goal. What do you want to do?
- Measurable: Can you measure your progress on reaching the goal?
- Achievable/Attainable/Actionable: Can you actually do it or identify someone who can help achieve it?
- Relevant/Realistic: Is it realistic? Are the actions your planning applicable to the goal (being busy does NOT mean being

productive, more on this in a moment)? Do you have what you need to complete the goal?.

• Time-bound: How long will it take to achieve this goal?

I want you to identify a project or a goal that you have in mind. Now, using the "SMART" goal, break up the goal into parts, and think of each step you will need to make in order to achieve your end goal. Remember, no matter how big your goal is, begin with the end in mind. But how does one do that? How can you plan for something you have no idea how to reach to begin with? This involves deconstruction.

Beyond the SMART Plan, Deconstruction

Deconstructing a plan requires some research on your part as well as some measure of humility. You never get the chance to see the struggles that somebody had to go through in order to get where they are now, whether it be becoming an online superstar or an executive at a major corporation. In spite of this, if the majority of the successful people whose examples you follow followed a path that was very similar to yours, it would not be unwise to do the same. In order to properly deconstruct a plan, one must first consider what steps have already been taken and then proceed in reverse order. Do not try to reinvent the wheel because very few people throughout history have been able to invent something new while also receiving credit for it. Start at the level of entry that you can achieve RIGHT NOW and work your way backwards from there. As soon as this is finished, you can start working on your SMART goal, which will help you advance to the next level of the development of your success. This is a thought experiment: Taking for granted that you have aspirations of playing basketball at the professional level. Your objective is attainable given that you stand at approximately 6 feet 7 inches, which is the standard height for a player. The professional players have an impressive level of athleticism and are very skilled when it comes to moving the ball around the court. They can make approximately 85% of their free throws. You are now officially familiar with the typical starting point. You are able to make 10 of every 20 attempts from behind the arc of the three-point line. Some days you will make more free throws than others, but on most days you should be able to make at least half of the attempts you make. You now have something to work off of, which is the baseline. Now you need to keep track of what part of the day you are working on to ensure that you have consistent results rather than just better days. Is there a connection between them? Do you feel that you perform better right after lunch or when you first get up in the morning? By answering these questions, you'll gain insight into the areas in which you have more room for improvement as well as those in which you excel. If working out for five hours every day leads to an increase in your number of consistent free throw shots to 12 out of 20 after a period of six weeks, then you are on the right path to achieve your goals. If you are not getting results, you need to look at what you are doing incorrectly and figure out how to fix it. Collaborate with a coach who can both teach you new things and encourage you to try new things. This is the next step in the execution of your SMART goal. But you shouldn't set your sights on becoming a professional player; rather, you should focus on reaching the required level. The next "SMART" goal steps consist of attempting to achieve professional status, how to get noticed and recruited, and so on once you have completed that goal and are ready to move on to the next step. But if you can't keep your attention on the task at hand, none of this will matter. If your objective is to earn a higher position at work, launch a business, or earn a profession, then you should concentrate on achieving that objective. One of the most challenging aspects of goal-setting is maintaining focus and keeping the destination in mind at all times. When you have days where you start to have doubts, which you will have, you need to remind yourself in a variety of ways from time to time. These days are inevitable. Putting it in writing is a step that can be very encouraging and I would argue, necessary.

A reflective journal is the status that is most applicable to the majority of situations. I am not referring to the kind of diary entry that says, "Dear Diary, I had a nice day today." Rather, I am referring to a physical book in which you record the steps you have taken to move closer to achieving your objective. You could be busy looking up information about the subject of your goal, which you may already be familiar with but have doubts about due to insecurity. Alternatively, you could be busy working out at a gym for five hours with 15 minute rests in between sets because you are focused on socializing, with no real objective on why you went to the gym other than to be active. To put it another way, just because you are active or busy does not mean that you are also productive. Keeping a journal for introspective purposes can be helpful at this point. When you take even a short amount of time out of your day (to be honest, I don't care if it's a document on your phone while you're sitting on the toilet) and truly reflect on what you have done to move closer to your goals in life, you begin to hold yourself accountable for your actions. You start to realize that each choice you make will have some effect on the achievement of your ultimate objective. One of my goals in life is to compete in and win a male bodybuilding competition at some point in the future. I didn't use the word "goal" because, despite the fact that I put in a lot of work at the gym, I just can't bring myself to give up sweets. It is possible for me to achieve my objective, but doing so would render the plans I outlined earlier to be impossible.

When setting goals using the SMART method, it is important not to overlook the "R." There is a finite number of time slots available throughout the day. You need to maintain realism and concentration. As a result, I put in a lot of effort at the gym because I care about my health and because research has shown that doing so can improve cognitive function. In order for me to make progress toward the goals I've set for my life, I need my brain to continue to operate normally. In addition, I make it a point to learn as much as I can about a variety of subjects within history, civics, education, current affairs, and politics in order to better prepare myself for the long-term objectives. I never stop working on my long-term objectives, both directly and indirectly. Be productive, not just active. In addition to reading this incredible book, what else are you doing to move yourself closer to achieving the things you want to accomplish? What kind of an appetite do you have to get what you want? This calls for more introspection and consideration on your part. People can say that they want to be lawyers and even make goals and plans to get there, but that doesn't mean they have any real interest in the field. On the other hand, they might have a strong interest in something like cooking. They can spend the entire day in the kitchen, researching and experimenting with new recipes. Now, let's say that an individual decides to become an attorney rather than a gourmet chef; what are the chances that they will be successful in that role? That is truly unquantifiable; however, what about resiliency in the face of adversity? Who is more likely to thrive despite the pressure and persistent conflict that life has a tendency to throw at people on a regular basis? When it comes down to it, the person who wants something the most is typically the one who will pick themselves up after being thrown into the mud.

The ability to determine "who really wants it" is a skill that has been honed to perfection by the United States Navy SEALS, the United States Army Ranger School, and the United States Army Special Forces. They receive severe abuse on all fronts, including the physical, the mental, and the emotional. They provide those who are participating with the opportunity to withdraw from the trial at any time, and the vast majority eventually accept this offer. The majority of actors forgo leading a life of luxury in exchange for the chance to be successful in acting. If you are not hungry for what you want, the process of pursuing your goal and dealing with the challenges you will encounter along the way can become tedious. You might even start being active just so you can feel like you're getting something done, but the truth is that because you're exhausted, you're not actually getting anything done—you're just being active. Because of this, you need to keep your hunger for the goal you have set for yourself. Always remember to keep your hunger, plan your goals using the "SMART" goal platform, deconstruct your dreams into reality, remain focused using whatever means are convenient for you, and plan!

Questions

1. What were the three key takeaways from the chapter?
2. What were the main arguments made in the chapter?
3. How could the ideas presented in the chapter be used to solve a particular problem or challenge you are facing?
4. How did the author support their arguments with evidence?
5. Create a SMART plan that will only take one week for you to accomplish. Name it, write it down, and begin that process immediately.

VI

Chapter 6: Inferring Possible Outcomes

"Those who have knowledge, don't predict. Those who predict, don't have knowledge."

—LAO TZU

During our time spent studying language arts, mathematics, and science in primary school, we are instructed on how to forecast particular outcomes based on the information that is presented to us. We read a passage and make an educated guess as to what will occur to the main character of the story, determine the answers based on equations that you are already familiar with, or determine a hypothesis based on our analysis to assess whether or not our presumptions are accurate. But what about the way you normally live your life? Is it feasible for someone to forecast potential outcomes based on the circumstances? It's possible that there are psychics among us, and I won't say whether or not I believe that to be true because other individuals have that belief. But, this does not preclude the potential of acquiring the abilities necessary to forecast the possibilities through research and the development of an unreliable intuition. This is a career held by a wide variety of people, including military generals, physicians, attorneys, investment brokers and agents, and even professional gamblers. The question that arises as a result of this is, how can you improve this ability to use in your day-to-day life? How can people who are good at critical thinking improve their ability to forecast events and take risks?

This form of "foresight" is more logical than it is superstitious. As was discussed before, abductive reasoning is an essential component in the process of outcome prediction. Let us not forget that this is a form of logical hypothesis, an observation or series of observations, and ultimately aims to identify the simplest and most plausible conclusion that can be drawn from the observations. Let us also not forget that. Predictions based on abduction almost always have an element of uncertainty or question, but they are treated as representing the best available or most likely conclusion. By conducting research on the relevant historical events and logical processes, we can improve these forecasts. This ability takes time and demands a high level of care and attention. This is a talent that many professionals struggle with for a variety of reasons, including an excessive belief in their own abilities, an oversimplification of reasoning and/or difficulties, and an overestimation of their own judgment and/or belief. Yet, the contrary is also true, which results in disappointment. Before we continue talking about how you can create this "foresight" for yourself, let's look at how this works in practice with a few different professions. It is best to examine what the professionals do, what they have in common, and then what practices may be made in your life to harness any skill. After doing this, it is possible to determine what it takes to harness any skill. Now before we get started on this project, I'd like for you all to keep in mind something that Norman Vincent Peale famously said: "Shoot for the moon. Even if you are unsuccessful, you will find yourself among the stars.

First, we will conduct an assessment of the generals and leaders of the armed forces. Each and every choice they make will either save or take the lives of soldiers. Not only do they need an understanding of the battlefield, its topography, and the capabilities of their forces, but they also need an understanding of the strengths and vulnerabilities of their adversaries. A good commander would be aware that once they have a complete understanding of the environment and the armies of both sides, the next steps would be to evaluate how to proceed and predict possible outcomes. This is because once they have a complete understanding of the environment and the armies, they can move on to the next step. A great number of generals look to the past for clues as to what will happen in the future and attempt to model their actions after past victories. On the other hand, they need to be careful not to use references that are not pertinent because doing so can damage your outcome. The generals of the German Nazi party were aware of the history of World War I, especially since many were veterans of that war. After suffering a previous defeat, these veterans of World War I came to the realization that they needed to improve their performance by avoiding repeating their earlier errors. The "Atlantic Wall" that the Nazis constructed was inspired by the "trench battle" that occurred during World War I. Yet, they failed to comprehend both their adversaries and their allies, in addition to the capabilities of each. Despite the fact that this would have been effective during World War I, the fact remains that this was a new conflict fought with new technology and new types of warriors. The result of this was that their Atlantic defenses were defeated on D-Day. Concerning their eastern front, they demonstrated a lack of environmental awareness when they attempted to breach the German-Soviet Non-Aggression Pact and invaded the Soviet Union. This led to disastrous results. They committed the same error that Napoleon Bonaparte did, which was to misjudge not just the terrain but also the weather and the will of the Russian people (harsh environments are not for the weak). In the end, the historical information that the German commanders relied on was selective, and they utilized past precedents that were not relevant to the situation. In a nutshell, the answer is that not everything can be suitable with every single circumstance. On the other hand, one may argue the contrary if the history in question was not selective but rather pertinent.

American Generals in the 1990s were not so careless and learned from the Nazis. To elaborate, the Nazis were lousy historians but amazing inventors during their time in power. Nobody wants to admit that the Nazis were responsible for anything we benefit now from or that they taught us anything valuable (more on this in Case Studies). However, during Operation Desert Storm (1990-1991), U.S. Army General Norman Schwarzkopf Jr. utilized a "blitzkrieg" strategy that was developed by the Nazis and lasted for a period of six weeks. This strategy involved launching rapid attacks against the enemy with mobile, maneuverable forces supported by tanks and air power. The terrain, which was desert, was very fitting for this use of tactics, and at the time, Iraq had superior numbers versus the American allies, so maneuverability was key because all trained fighters know that if the opponent is larger, you need to out skill and outmaneuver them to win. The eventual result of Operation Desert Storm was the most one-sided victory that has ever been achieved in modern warfare. The infrastructure of Iraq was leveled, and their military was utterly decimated, by the United States. Now obviously, there were still more lessons to be learned; however, the prediction of General Schwarzkopf, Jr.'s success was based on several factors, including the risk-reward analysis, the clear purpose of the mission, and the predictability of the outcome based on abductive reasoning by using historical evidence as the case studies. Now obviously, there were still more lessons to be learned.

Nazi's were very successful in military warfare until:

1. They began to believe they were invincible; believing your own propaganda, believing in your (non-existing) immortality, is usually the main cause of death for empires.
2. They felt morally superior; they chose to kill more jews rather than reinforce their armies.

3. They outstretched themselves; history of warfare clearly shows you cannot have two or more major armies in two separate fronts without severe consequences.

If they had done proper research on history and not believed that "their crap don't stink," as I like to say when I'm with my friends, the results would have been different and potentially terrifying. Yet, generals are able to forecast outcomes the majority of the time when they use the Art of War in conjunction with historical evidence. But what about those who work in other fields?

In a certain respect, the professions of Doctor and Lawyer are somewhat comparable to one another. Case studies are utilized by both of them in order to examine, understand, and determine how to handle various scenarios. When you go to the doctor, he or she will evaluate your symptoms, as well as any deficits and discomforts you may be experiencing. It's possible that, depending on your level of experience, you'll need to collect data from the patient, draw conclusions from those facts, and then communicate those findings to the senior or supervisory physicians. At the end, considering all of the evidence that were obtained, they hypothesize by employing abductive reasoning, and administer the prescription with a foreseeable result that has risks that are tolerable. In both courtroom and legal contexts, lawyers perform the same functions. The complaints, defects, and aches and pains experienced by their customers have a connection to the law. Whenever a client is injured because of an automobile accident, the attorney needs to investigate the location where the accident took place, the time when it occurred, the weather, what the client was wearing, what the driver was doing, and any other conceivable detail that is accessible. They do this not because they are attempting to discover a solution but rather because they are trying to gather sufficient evidence against the driver that will allow for the least amount of rebuttals that are available. They draw up possible conclusions and outcomes (settlement and counter-settlements), and then report to senior legal partners in their respective firms to share their findings and evaluate any loopholes. Depending on their level of experience, they continue to use methods that are analogous to those used by doctors. These methods include, but are not limited to, hypothesizing, conducting experiments and testing hypotheses through debates and arguments with other legal partners.

These approaches, which are used in both fields, are based on an adaptation of the scientific method as well as abductive logic. Both medical professionals and legal representatives will look at case studies that are pertinent to their circumstances in order to achieve a consistent outcome. It is possible for a medical professional to cause the death of a patient or to be held legally liable for medical malpractice if they incorrectly interpret a case study that is not applicable to the circumstances of the patient's condition or if they are overly confident in their diagnosis. On the other hand, attorneys will lose more cases, which might lead to fewer opportunities for advancement in their respective careers. In the event that they are criminal lawyers who defend clients who may be innocent, there is a good chance that they will spend time for a crime that they did not commit. In spite of this, increasing the use of inductive reasoning along with the various components of the scientific process results in a more likely outcome. This translates to a greater chance of accomplishment for professionals such as doctors and lawyers. Those who work as traders on Wall Street display the same skills in risk assessment and anticipating outcomes in their daily employment. Abductive reasoning has the potential to be an analytical tool in the field of finance. They make use of fundamental analysis, technical analysis, and investment analysis in various forms. Traders and analysts conduct research on a company's balance sheets, financial ratios, and other types of data linked to the company's growth and future as part of the process known as fundamental analysis. Traders and analysts examine the trend of the markets, the sector in which it operates, and attempt to forecast the movement of stocks and bonds using technical analysis. Hypothetical situations are examined using historical data, current market patterns, and projected future growth rates in the context of investment analysis.

Nonetheless, each and every one of these is an example of abductive reasoning logic. If the results of these three evaluations could be relied upon, then the traders would consistently employ that particular method. On the other hand, fundamental, technical, and investment analysis can produce more accurate forecasts of future events if and only if they are carried out in the correct manner. If investors and traders make the same errors in judgment that were made by the Generals, Physicians, and Attorneys that we discussed previously, they will also end up in the same position, which is failure. What then is it that we can take away from these careers that we can use in our everyday lives? You need to come to a conclusion using abductive reasoning whenever you examine a scenario in your life, whether it concerns personal connections, professional endeavors, or significant life choices. Gather all available facts and identify possible outcomes. Because of this, it is necessary for the premises to be mainly accurate in order for the conclusion to be accurate. The facts that you are witnessing will determine what those premises are, thus it all hinges on those facts. Do you just take that person's word for it if you're trying to figure out whether they're a cheater and it's someone you're interested in romantically? If they have a history, what are their justifications for cheating, and how many justifications have they used in the past? Your choice on whether or not to be in a relationship with that person ought to take this into consideration, as it should. In addition, to what extent are you willing to put yourself in harm's way? In order to decide whether or not your decision is appropriate, what other "case studies" can you analyze? Do you have a family member or a close friend who has taken decisions that are analogous to your own, and you are unhappy with the results?

The instances that are all around you have the potential to serve as case studies that will assist you in making an abductively logical judgment. According to research conducted by psychologists, those who come from abusive families have a much increased risk of entering into abusive relationships themselves (and sometimes be the abuser, regardless of gender). In the case of divorces, the same principle applies. Make the experiences that are occurring around you into the case studies that you can learn from rather than letting them become the "rhyme" that is repeated in the history of your family. The same is true for one's professional path. It is important to seek information and history not only from people who have achieved success but also from people who have experienced failure. Make use of the people's experiences as examples of what to do and what not to do as case studies. Purchasing and managing your own home? Find friends, family members, and other people online who have purchased homes of a comparable type, listen to their grievances, and determine whether or not they are pertinent. After doing so, create abductively logical choices that are supported by the case studies.

Steps for predictive analysis

Observation

The act of observation comes at the beginning of the process of critical thinking used for predictive analysis. This requires collecting information, which can be done either through direct observation or through the use of secondary sources. The most important thing is to try to be as objective as possible and to refrain from making snap judgments based on information that is either incomplete or prejudiced. Throughout this stage of the process, your primary focus should be on gathering as much information as possible, and you should make a note of any facts, figures, or data that are pertinent to the issue at hand.

Analysis

Following the completion of the step in which you gather information, the following step is to analyze the data. This requires segmenting the material into smaller bits, recognizing patterns and relationships, and searching for any inconsistencies or contradictions that may exist. You will be able to acquire a more in-depth grasp of the facts as well as discover any potential issues or areas of worry thanks to this stage. In this stage of the process, your attention should be focused on locating the underlying reasons, recognizing any patterns or trends, and gaining an understanding of how the knowledge pertains to the issue at hand.

Interpretation and Evaluation

After that, you would proceed to the next step, which is the evaluation, during which you would create an opinion regarding the value or significance of the information. This would entail taking a look at the evidence, determining the plausibility of the arguments, and weighing the reliability of the sources. For instance, if you were the manager, you would evaluate the project proposal by determining whether or not the project has a good chance of being successful, determining whether or not the project is feasible, and considering the amount of money and resources that will be required to carry out the project.

Inference

Following the conclusion of the analysis of the data, the next and last phase is to draw conclusions based on the information. After the previous steps of information collection, analysis, interpretation, and evaluation, you will now move on to the stage of drawing conclusions and making decisions based on the data you have gathered. For instance, as a manager, you might draw the conclusion that the project proposal presents a good opportunity for the business and choose to move forward with it. Alternatively, you might draw the conclusion that there are too many potential pitfalls and drawbacks and choose to turn down the proposal. It is essential to keep in mind that the process of critical thinking is not a one-time occurrence; rather, it is an iterative process, and you may find that you need to return to earlier steps in order to acquire additional knowledge or reassess your decision.

Discovering case studies that are applicable to your requirements can be the determining factor in your ability to forecast the results of various scenarios. For instance, the fact that someone did not receive acceptance to a specific university because they did not perform well in any of their high school classes is irrelevant to the success of an individual in elementary school. However, if you are someone who has already been accepted to the university that you want to attend, has participated in volunteer work, and has maintained grades high enough to get a letter of recommendation from the principal or dean of your school, then repeating these steps may give you the same or similar results. The same principle applies to choosing a particular line of work or advancing in one's current position. If you want the position of your supervisor, you should find out what they did to get promoted and emulate their success. Have they received a degree or a certification for their work? If that's the case, what other aspects of their operation led to their success? Were they the first ones to enter the workplace and the last ones to leave it? Have they conducted any research into potential ways to boost productivity, profits, or employee morale? In spite of this, if the supervisor didn't deserve the promotion because of some questionable behavior, you should look for other examples that are consistent with your moral principles and can serve as a model for you to follow. As you get more proficient in this ability, you will start to develop an instinct that is almost identical to the concept of "foresight." This is due to the fact that you are cultivating wisdom, something that is exceedingly uncommon in the 21st century. Individuals who are considered to be intelligent are sometimes regarded as those who have a mysteriously accurate sense of foresight. That is not something you develop in any academic setting but rather through the simple accumulation of experience. But, given that you are not eternal, you are required to gain knowledge not only from your own experiences but also from those of other people. If you can start to take in the

lessons that are going on around you, you can start to make more accurate predictions about the probable outcomes. Wisdom can be gained
at any point in life; there is no age at which it is impossible to do so.
The procedure entails performing an organized analysis of the data and
arriving at conclusions that are supported by sufficient evidence. The
steps of observation, analysis, interpretation, evaluation, and inference
are involved in the process. It is possible for managers and critical
thinkers to develop their capacity to forecast outcomes and make decisions based on sound information if they follow this method.

Questions

1. How does the process of observing help make sure that the results of predictive analysis are correct?
2. How does the step of analyzing the data help find discrepancies and contradictions?
3. What criteria should be used in evaluating the reliability of the sources of information in the process of critical thinking?
4. How can the process of inference be used to make decisions based on data gathered through observation, analysis, interpretation, and evaluation?
5. How can looking at case studies help you predict what will happen and decide what to do in a certain situation?

VII

Chapter 7: Influence Using Rhetoric and the Power of Words

"A newspaper is not only a collective propagandist and a collective agitator, it is also a collective organizer."

—VLADIMIR LENIN[3]

The use of rhetorical tactics to exert control over a group of individuals possesses a sinister and fascinating quality all at once. In the 21st century, vast volumes of propaganda are spread across our media, and they also make use of hyperbole in order to provide credence to their facts, despite the fact that they do not employ any FACTS. Unfortunately, the vast majority of people are either unaware of this or are unable to adequately describe the term "rhetoric" or the power that it possesses.

Rhetorical tactics are used in a variety of contexts, including elections, the news, commercial advertising, the government, the media, and organizations. And the best way to comprehend it is to first describe it and then study how it is used on you. This is the greatest approach to comprehend it. Pathos, Logos, and Ethos are the three concepts that Aristotle, the famed ancient Greek philosopher who lived from 384 BC to 322 BC, used to characterize rhetoric:

1. Pathos: The Emotional Appeal (Pull the emotional strings)
2. Logos: The Logical Appeal ("facts", Logic, etc.)
3. Ethos: Appeal to Credibility (Convince the audience the "seller" can be trusted)

Most advertisements and propaganda will use a minimum of two out of the three (three being the most effective yet most difficult to pull off). Let's examine these examples:

1. An advertisement for a sports drink, you see a famous athlete performing, they are vigorously exerting themselves to the point of exhaustion before pausing to swallow a refreshing beverage. (which they hold conveniently showing the logo). You have experienced Ethos and possibly Pathos, if you appreciate the sport or the athlete.
2. An elected official describes a group of Hispanic people who are part of an organized crime syndicate as animals for their cruelty to other people. The media begins an outcry of rage, crying and stating "how could he say that Hispanics are animals?!" They invite experts to discuss how deplorable this elected official is and the correlation between Hispanics and animals.
3. A cigarette company publishes an ad in a magazine stating Physicians/Dentists approve a particular company over the other. This is an example of Logos and Ethos because the seller is not only trusted but they are stating a "fact".
   ◦ Note: This was a normal strategy used in the 1930s and 1940s to not only support the industry, but to find new smokers. You can also experience this a step further using

all three forms of rhetoric in the films that were created at the time[4].

How does the third case fit into all three categories? Pathos was employed by the group in the form of simple emotional outbursts. We are humans, and the vast majority of humans with developed social abilities have a response when they witness other humans in pain. In Logos, they stated the truth that the elected official DID say "Hispanics...animals" but neglected and manipulated all other facts which would have changed the context. And finally, Finally, they want legal scholars, social scientists, and advocates for civil rights to back the argument that the elected official did say "Hispanics are animals." The majority of people would be offended if you only noticed the latter. And as a Hispanic, I would too. The application of analytical and deductive reasoning is required here. Critical thinkers won't pass judgment until they have all the relevant information and can determine whether or not they were manipulated in any way. Rhetoric has been utilized as the basis for the names of programs developed by other groups that pursue completely distinct goals. One example would be "The Final Solution" which was Nazi Germany's plan for a "better future" and "solve the German problem" by trying to exterminate an entire race of people (Jewish people). Despite the fact that they were unsuccessful (which is a relief), they were nevertheless able to kill 2.7 million people. Another illustration of this would be "The Great Leap Forward," which was part of the Chinese Communist revolution and was responsible for the deaths of 20–46 million people[5] [6] [7]. These are simply two of Numerous instances that come to mind when thinking about history; however, let's shift our attention and evaluate contemporary events as well as the many political and civil rights activists in the 21st century that utilize similar rhetorical strategies.

Case Study

The phrase "black lives matter" is likely to elicit an emotional response (referred to as "Pathos") from those who encounter it. There are now a number of organizations and movements that make use of the phrase "black lives matter," but each of them pursues a unique set of goals (and some are intertwined). One organization will present itself as an anti-racism movement, another will claim to be anti-police and advocates of the murders of black people at the hands of law enforcement, and the third will be an organization composed of trained Marxists who want to reconstruct an entire society[8]. Which one of these three uses the term in a way that contradicts what the title says it will be used for? The accusation that the founders of the Black Lives Matter organization are trained Marxists has already been stated by those who founded the organization. To provide further clarification, Karl Marx, one of the authors of the Communist Manifesto, believed that socialism was an essential stepping stone toward communism[9]. Thus, by making use of "Deductive Reasoning" logic (for example: "All humans are mortal. Julie is a person. This means that Julie will eventually die "), which many people argue is the most accurate way of measuring logic, Karl Marx wrote that Socialism is the way to "utopia." Karl Marx also wrote that Socialism is a key step to communism. As a result, Karl Marx believed that the only way to "utopia" is through communism. In addition, if you have training in Marxism, you have training in communism as well[10]. As a side note, as of the time of this writing, the particular organization in question has not finished the process of registering as a non-profit, which means that they are exempt from the legal requirement to disclose what they intend to do with the money that they have been given. Despite this, they have been successful in raising well over one hundred and twenty million dollars as of the time this article was written, and they also have the backing and support of a different charitable organization known as "Thousand Currents" [11]. This is not uncommon. On the other hand, the fact that the Black Lives Matter movement prioritizes communism over genuine human lives raises a lot of doubts about the organization's priorities. Yet if there is one thing that is certain, it is that the amount of money provided by individuals and organizations in the United States was unparalleled. This clearly shows the following logical conclusions:

1. If most Americans and organizations donated to "Black Lives Matter" because they believe in the name and fully support the idea that all black lives do matter (as it should!).
2. The name and rhetoric suggests they are against racism.
3. Therefore, most Americans are against racism.

This unfortunate separation of ideology distorts the vision of racism on people of color. Because of this, we lose sight of more important things such as overall racism and black on black crime which is by far the largest cause of death to any young black males[12]. Unfortunately, many far-left leaning people use the Lenin tactic of "ad hominem", which is the attack of a person rather than their opinions/arguments (Demonizing) and "fallacies" (undermine the logic of your argument with common errors in reasoning), which is documented in detail in the "Two Tactics of Social-Democracy in the Democratic Revolution"[13]. And most people will not realize they are using a strategy from Lenin. (Update: As of 2023, BLM has been allegedly under several investigations from the Internal Revenue Service in the United States around 2022[121] and has reorganized, according to several news sources in 2023[119]. Moreover, there has been an expose produced by the Daily Wire entitled The Greatest Lie Ever Sold[120] that has a different perspective on the organization.)

What's In a Name?

Why would a company want to manipulate your feelings with a name in the first place? Why would you try to conceal your goals by using a name that has nothing to do with what you're trying to accomplish? These are questions that only you can answer, but I have a sneaking suspicion that they do not want you to know the truth for one simple reason: they do not want you to find out. This is a game in which you use your feelings to earn credibility and gain influence over others. This can also be seen on the internet. When you consider how "click bait" works on social media and how it uses your emotions to entice you to click on such images as those with headlines that read "You will never believe what this famous celeb did!" or "I can't believe how easy it is to make this much money!" there is an immediate call to action to click on the link. The moment you click on one of their links, they have automatically made cash from the advertisements on those pages, but all you will receive is useless information. Because of this, it is essential to make use of reasoning before resorting to supporting rhetoric and words with their literal meaning. Until you take the effort to investigate the "why" and locate the logic in the situation (Deductive reasoning can lead to an absolutely true conclusion if and only if the premises that lead to that conclusion are also true.). If you do this, the facts that you find will support your truth provided that they are congruent with it. Be wary of persons who employ rhetoric to make a claim, as well as the words they choose. Look at how the Nazis used the power of words to try to eradicate an entire race, or how communism led to the annihilation of MILLIONS of people over the world. Both of these ideologies exploited the power of words. When you can utilize elegant language to make your point, it is much simpler to convince groups of people to do what you want them to.

Questions

1. Reflect on Rhetoric: Look for 3 ads that you find interesting. Examine the ads and discuss or write down what strategies they were using to influence you.

- Based on your findings, is there a correlation? Are the ads similar? Is the rhetoric similar?
- NOTE: If you find a correlation on what influences you, you may have found a personal softness within a particular form of rhetoric (and that's ok! We will evaluate that in a later chapter.).

2. Question: How can you define Rhetoric in your own words? Reflect on a time you may have used rhetoric in your own personal life.

3. Small Project-Based Practice: You need to influence someone to do something you want. It can be anything (Give you money? Buy you something? See things your way?): Think of a strategy on how you can use rhetoric to your advantage.

- TIP: Are they emotional? Are they fact driven? Do they trust you? By answering these questions before using the strategy, you can figure out which form of rhetoric to use. However, please remember, more is better.

PART THREE

Identifying and
Evaluating
Arguments

VIII

❦

Chapter 8: Identifying and Evaluating Arguments

"Great leaders are almost always great simplifiers, who can cut through argument, debate and doubt, to offer a solution everybody can understand."

—COLIN POWELL

Finding and evaluating different arguments is a significant component of having the ability to think critically. An argument is a set of claims, one of which is the conclusion. The conclusion relies on the other claims, often known as premises, to provide support for or explanation of the conclusion. Locating arguments and evaluating how compelling they are are essential steps in the process of determining which assertions are true and which are not. This chapter will provide you with an overview of how to recognize arguments and the various types of arguments that you may encounter, as well as recommendations and tactics for determining the validity of the arguments that you encounter.

An argument's purpose is to convince the audience that the proposed conclusion is justified by the evidence presented in the premises of the argument. In order to think critically about an argument, you need to be able to recognize the argument's conclusion, its premises, and its validity. To put this another way, you need to be able to determine whether or not the premises are correct, whether or not the conclusion logically follows from the premises, and whether or not the argument contains any logical fallacies.

If you are familiar with the concept of an argument, it will be much simpler for you to recognize one when you hear it presented in a text, a speech, an advertisement for a political candidate, a personal view, or even in an everyday discussion. As soon as you understand what an argument is, you will be able to decide whether or not it is beneficial. A strong argument adheres to the rules of logic and is founded on solid premises. A weak argument is one that is either illogical or that is based on faulty premises. The ability to identify and analyze different lines of reasoning is an essential component of critical thinking. This enables you to differentiate between assertions that are believable and those that are not reliable, to reason effectively, and to arrive at sound decisions.

Identifying Arguments

There are two parts to an argument: the conclusion and the premises (points you're making). The conclusion is the claim that the person making the argument wants you to agree with, and the premises are the reasons or pieces of evidence that support the claim. To figure out what an argument is, you need to know both the conclusion and the premises. Here are some tips and strategies for identifying arguments:

1. Look for keywords and phrases such as "therefore," "hence," "so," "because," "due to," "since," "as a result," which indicate the presence of an argument.

Example: "I failed my math test *because* I didn't study enough"

In this sentence, "because" indicate that there's an argument being made and the claim being made is "I failed my math test" and the reason/premise for that is "I didn't study enough"

2. Identify the main claim or point that the speaker or writer is trying to make. This is likely to be the conclusion.

   Example: In a political speech, the speaker might say "We need to invest in more renewable energy sources in order to combat climate change" The main claim or point the speaker is trying to make is "We need to invest in more renewable energy sources"

3. Look for evidence or reasons that are offered to support the main claim. These are likely to be the premises.

   Example: In the previous example, "in order to combat climate change" is the evidence or reason provided to support the main claim "We need to invest in more renewable energy sources"

4. Be aware that arguments can be implicit rather than explicit, so it's important to be on the lookout for arguments even when they are not clearly labeled as such.

Example: An advertisement for a product that only shows happy customers using the product without explicitly stating "buy our product, it will make you happy too"

Types of Arguments

There are several different types of arguments that you may encounter:

Deductive arguments: A form of logical argument known as a deductive argument seeks to prove its conclusion with absolute certainty by demonstrating that the conclusion necessarily follows from the premises presented in the argument.

In a deductive argument, the premises offer evidence or support for the conclusion, and it is asserted that the conclusion logically follows on from the premises. While using deductive reasoning, the most important thing to keep in mind is that if the premises are true, then the conclusion must also be true. For example, consider the following deductive argument:

Premise 1: All mammals are warm-blooded.
Premise 2: Dogs are mammals.
Conclusion: Therefore, dogs are warm-blooded.

In this argument, the evidence for the conclusion comes from the two premises. If we agree that all mammals have warm blood, and if we also agree that dogs are mammals, then it follows that dogs must have warm blood. If the premises are true, then the conclusion must also be true.

Deductive reasoning is often used in math, science, and philosophy, and it is often used to make arguments that are thought to be logically sound. But it's important to remember that deductive arguments are only as strong as their premises, and if the premises are false, the argument can be wrong even if the reasoning is good.

Inductive arguments: Inductive arguments try to show that a conclusion is true with strong evidence, but they don't prove that the conclusion is true. Inductive arguments use generalizations based on what the person has seen or done.
In an inductive argument, the premises give evidence that makes it more likely that the conclusion is true, but they don't prove it. For example, if we see a large number of black crows, we might assume that all crows are black. This generalization isn't sure to be true, though, because we might not have seen every kind of crow yet.
Depending on how good the evidence is, an inductive argument can be strong or weak. A strong inductive argument gives evidence that makes it very likely that the conclusion is true. A weak inductive argument, on the other hand, only gives weak evidence.

It's important to remember that inductive arguments are different from deductive arguments, which try to guarantee the truth if the premises are true. In a deductive argument, the premises are supposed to show that the conclusion is true, while in an inductive argument, the premises only show that the conclusion is more likely to be true.

Overall, inductive arguments are a useful tool for reasoning and making decisions because they let us draw conclusions based on what we know and have seen. But it's important to use critical thinking to figure out how good the evidence is and to know what inductive reasoning can't do.

Abductive arguments: A type of reasoning called "inference to the best explanation" is when a conclusion is made based on the best explanation. Abductive reasoning, on the other hand, doesn't lead to a conclusion that must be true, but rather to a plausible explanation.

In an abductive argument, the conclusion is drawn from the available evidence and the most likely explanation for that evidence. The strength of the argument depends on how likely the explanation is, how important and good the evidence is, and whether or not there are other, more likely explanations.

For example, if you come home and find that your front door is broken, your window is smashed, and your valuables are gone, the best explanation is that your home was broken into. Even though we don't know for sure that this is what happened, based on what we know, this is the most likely explanation.

Abductive arguments can be used in science, law, and even making decisions in everyday life. They let us make decisions based on the information we have and the most likely explanation. But it's important to remember that the plausibility of an explanation is a matter of opinion and can change depending on the person and their own biases. So, it's important to think about different possible explanations and look at the evidence in an unbiased way.

Cogent arguments: A strong argument with true premises makes a cogent argument. A strong argument is one in which the truth of the premises makes it likely that the conclusion is also true. A true premise is one that matches reality. Two things must be true for an argument to make sense. First, the premises have to be either true or very likely to be true. Second, the premises need to be related to the conclusion, which means they need to back up the conclusion.

In order to think critically, we need to be able to tell the difference between good and bad arguments. A convincing argument is more likely to be logically sound, which means that the premises are true and the conclusion makes sense when you look at them together. A weak or fallacious argument, on the other hand, is less likely to be a good one. It may be based on false premises or have logical mistakes.

When judging arguments, it's important to think about whether or not they make sense. If an argument makes sense, it is more likely to be convincing and should be given more weight. On the other hand, if an argument doesn't make sense, it should be looked at with skepticism, and it may be necessary to look into it more to see if it's true.

Non-cogent arguments: non-cogent arguments are arguments that fail to provide good reasons for accepting their conclusions. Unlike cogent arguments, non-cogent arguments are not rationally compelling and may contain various types of errors, such as fallacies, false premises, or unsupported assumptions.

There are many kinds of arguments that don't make sense (non-cogent), but some common ones are emotional appeals, appeals to authority, attacks on the person making the argument, straw man arguments, and false dichotomies. These arguments may be persuasive to some people, but they do not provide good reasons for accepting their conclusions. It is important to be able to identify non-cogent arguments so that you can avoid being swayed by faulty reasoning.

Evaluating Arguments

Once you've identified an argument, the next step is to evaluate its soundness. Here are some tips and strategies for evaluating arguments:

1. Check if the premises are true: The soundness of an argument depends on the truth of the premises, so it's important to evaluate the evidence and see if it supports the conclusion or not.
   Example: In the argument " Eating organic food is better for the environment because organic farming practices are less harmful to the environment", you would need to evaluate the truth of the premise "organic farming practices are less harmful to the environment" by looking at studies or expert opinions.

2. Look for logical fallacies: Logical fallacies are errors in reasoning that can make an argument unsound. Examples include ad hominem attacks, appeals to emotion, and strawman arguments.
   Example: "You can't trust anything that scientist says, they're all just in it for the money" this is an ad hominem attack and it's a logical fallacy, rather than addressing the argument, it attacks the person who's making it.

3. Check for consistency and coherence: Make sure that the conclusion and the premises are consistent and that the argument as a whole is coherent.
   Example: "Eating meat is bad for your health because it's high in cholesterol, but you should eat meat because it's high in protein" In this case the argument is not coherent, the premises contradicts each other, it's not possible to have an argument that concludes that something is bad and good at the same time.

4. Consider alternative explanations: Be open to alternative

explanations and consider whether there are other possible explanations for the evidence.

Example: In an argument "The increase in crime rate is due to the lack of police presence in the area", you would want to consider alternative explanations such as economic factors, social factors, etc before accepting the argument as sound.

Lastly, in any argument or debate, the definitions must be clear and precise. Any argument can lead to an unproductive debate if one has a different definition compared to another. You must understand the meaning of the words that are being used. Furthermore, you can become a more effective critical thinker by learning how to recognize arguments, and then evaluating those arguments. This ability will serve you well throughout your life because it is necessary in a variety of facets of life, including both your personal and professional lives.

Questions

1. Can you think of a recent situation in which you encountered an argument? How did you evaluate it?
2. How do you currently go about identifying arguments?
3. In what ways can identifying and evaluating arguments be beneficial to your personal and professional life?
4. Can you think of a time when an argument's conclusion was not true but the premise was true?
5. How can you improve your ability to identify and evaluate arguments?

IX

Chapter 9: Understanding Common Fallacies and How to Avoid Them

"Read not to contradict and confute; nor to believe and take for granted; nor to find talk and discourse; but to weigh and consider."

—FRANCIS BACON

In this section, we're going to dive into the world of common fallacies and explore how to avoid them. Fallacies are mistakes in reasoning that can lead us to believe something that isn't true or make decisions that aren't in our best interests. By learning about these mistakes and how to spot them, we can improve our ability to think critically and make better choices.

Ad Hominem Fallacy

In the realm of logic and argumentation, attacking the person making an argument instead of addressing the argument itself is known as an ad hominem fallacy. This fallacy is not only intellectually lazy but also highly counterproductive in advancing any fruitful discussion or debate. It's a common mistake that people make, whether they're talking about politics or posting on social media.

A person commits an ad hominem fallacy when they attack the character, motives, or other personal qualities of their opponent instead of dealing with the main points of their argument. For instance, if someone argues that increasing the minimum wage would benefit low-wage workers, and someone else responds by calling them a "socialist," "lazy," or "uninformed," they have committed an ad hominem fallacy. Another example can be when someone responds to an argument by attacking their race, gender, and/or background. This kind of attack is not only pointless, but it also doesn't help the other side's case that the minimum wage shouldn't go up.

One reason ad hominem attacks are so common is because they are easy to make. Attacking someone's character or credibility doesn't take much time or research, and it doesn't require critical thinking or the ability to persuade. It is also a lot easier to attack someone's character than to make a well-thought-out argument with good evidence. Ad hominem attacks are often the first resort of those who lack evidence or logical support for their own positions.

The ad hominem fallacy takes many forms, such as attacking someone's age, gender, race, education, social class, occupation, religion, political affiliation, or personal history. Attackers who use ad hominem try to discredit their opponents by focusing on their personal traits instead of addressing the validity of their arguments. These attacks can take on a variety of forms, from insults and ridicule to character assassination and even threats of violence.

Even though it is used a great deal, the ad hominem fallacy is a very terrible way to argue. It undermines the process of critical thinking and reasoned debate, as it substitutes personal attacks for reasoned discourse. It also distracts from the actual issue under discussion, as the focus shifts to the character and credibility of the people making the argument, rather than the argument itself. Ad hominem attacks can also hurt relationships and make it harder for people to trust each other. This makes it harder for people to come to an agreement or find common ground.

Strawman Fallacy

The strawman fallacy is a type of argumentative fallacy that happens when someone misrepresents or oversimplifies someone else's argument to make it easier to attack. This is a common way to derail an opponent's argument without actually addressing the issue. It is often used in debates and discussions.

The word "strawman" comes from the practice of using a straw man, or a lifeless dummy made of straw, as a target for practice or training. In the same way, a "straw man" argument is a version of an opponent's argument that doesn't make sense and is easy to attack.

The strawman fallacy usually happens when one person misrepresents the other person's argument in a way that makes it easier to argue against. For example, if two people are arguing about how to get rid of crime, one person might say that more police and harsher punishments will work. The other person might then use the straw man fallacy by saying something like, "Oh, so you think we should just throw everyone in jail and forget about rehabilitation?" This oversimplifies the original argument and makes it easier to argue against because it sounds like an extreme position.

There are a number of ways to keep from using the straw man fallacy. One way is to make sure you understand your opponent's point of view before you answer. This means taking the time to understand their point of view and not just responding to a simplified or exaggerated version of their argument.

You can also avoid the straw man fallacy by focusing on the real issue at hand instead of attacking a simplified or wrongly portrayed version of the argument. This means you should stay on topic and resist the urge to make a "straw man" to attack. It is important to know when you or someone else is using the straw man fallacy in an argument. By avoiding this mistaken idea, you can have more productive and useful conversations that help you understand the issues at hand better.

The Appeal to Emotion

As people, we often let our feelings guide us. The way we feel, whether it's happiness, anger, love, or hate, has a big impact on what we think and do. So, it shouldn't be a surprise that emotional appeals are often used in advertising, politics, and persuasion. An appeal to emotion is a type of argument that tries to get people to agree with a certain point of view or do a certain thing by appealing to their emotions.

Emotional appeals (Pathos) are powerful because they skip over our rational minds and go straight to our feelings. When we care about something emotionally, our minds are more open to the ideas and arguments that back it up. This is why ads use pictures of happy families or cute animals to sell their products, why politicians tell sad stories to get people to vote for them, and why charities use pictures of hurt children to get people to give money.

But it's not always a good thing to use emotional appeals. When used to trick or trick people, emotional appeals can be dangerous. Untrustworthy speakers can get us to do things that aren't in our best interests by playing on our fears, prejudices, or wants. For example, a politician might play on people's fears to get them to support a policy that is bad for them, or an advertiser might use images of sex and violence to sell products that might not be very good.

So, it's important to be aware of the ways that emotional appeals can be used to control us. By learning to spot the signs of emotional appeals, we can make ourselves less likely to be swayed by them. Using loaded language is one of the most common ways to try to get people to feel something. Words like "freedom," "justice," "equality," and "security" can make people feel strong emotions and make them act in strong ways. When these words are used in an argument to persuade us, we should take a step back and think about whether they are being used to trick us.

Using vivid images is another sign of an emotional appeal. When people talk about events or situations in a graphic way, they are often trying to get people to feel something. For instance, a politician might talk about how horrible a terrorist attack is to make us feel scared and helpless. By being aware of how vivid images can make us feel, we can become more critical of messages that try to persuade us.

Tu Quoque

Tu quoque is a form of logical fallacy that refers to the practice of diverting criticism or accusations by pointing out that the accuser is also guilty of the same or similar behavior. This can be done by arguing that both parties have engaged in the same or similar actions.

The line of reasoning typically goes as follows: "If you're acting in the same manner, I don't see why I shouldn't, either." or "What gives you the right to judge me when you've been guilty of the same thing yourself?"

For instance, if someone is accused of cheating on a test and their response is, "Well, you cheated on the prior test and didn't get caught, so why can't I?" (You cheated on the previous test and weren't detected, so why can't I?) This answer makes an effort to redirect attention away from the charge and toward the person making the accusation.

The fact that the accuser is also guilty of the behavior does not change the fact that the accused is still guilty of the behavior that was initially being accused of, even if it is true that the accuser is also guilty of the activity. Because it does not address the topic at hand and instead aims to discredit the accuser, the Tu Quoque fallacy is an example of a logical fallacy.

False Dilemma: Fallacy of Limited Choices

We often encounter what seems to be an either/or choice. But these choices aren't always mutually exclusive, and there are often many more choices than just these two. This is a common mistake that can lead us to make bad decisions. It is called a false dilemma or a false dichotomy.

When we think we only have two choices, but there are actually more, this is called a false dilemma. This fallacy is often used as a way to get people to choose one thing over another without giving them any other options. When someone gives us a choice between two things, they often do it in a way that makes one seem much better than the other. This makes us choose something we might not have otherwise.

The old "you're either with us or against us" argument is a good example of a false dilemma. Politicians often use this kind of argument to make people feel like they have to pick one side or the other. But this kind of thinking is wrong because it doesn't take into account the possibility that there is a third choice or that the two choices given are not the only ones.

The idea that we must either cut back on social services or raise taxes is another example of a false dilemma. This argument doesn't take into account the fact that there may be other ways to balance the budget, like cutting spending in other areas or finding new ways to make money. Because this argument only gives us two choices, it makes us feel like we have to choose between two bad options.

To avoid being stuck in a false dilemma, it's important to look for other choices and consider the possibility that you may have more options than you think. It is also important to look at the assumptions that are being made and to think about whether the choices that are being given are really the only ones.

Genetic Fallacy

The genetic fallacy is a type of logical fallacy that happens when you judge or argue about something based on its origins or history instead of judging it on its own merits or how it is right now. This kind of mistake is common in many fields, like politics, philosophy, and even science. It's important to be aware of this fallacy so you don't make bad arguments or come to wrong conclusions.

The word "genetic fallacy" comes from the Greek word "genesis," which means "beginning." This fallacy occurs when someone decides whether a claim is true or false based only on where it came from or how long it has been around. For example, someone might not agree with an argument because it comes from a certain person or group, or they might agree with it just because it has been around for a long time.

The ad hominem argument is a common example of the genetic fallacy. In this argument, someone attacks the person making the argument instead of the argument itself. This is a mistake because it doesn't look at the argument itself but at the person who is making it. The argument from tradition is another example. This is when someone says that something is true or important just because it has been done or believed for a long time.

To avoid the genetic fallacy, it's important to judge arguments on their own merits and not based on where they came from or how long they've been around. This means paying attention to the content of the argument and judging it based on how well it makes sense, what evidence it has, and how well it fits with the topic at hand. Also, it's important not to attack people who are arguing or to only use tradition to back up an argument.

There are many more fallacies to watch out for, but the most important thing is to look at every argument critically and be willing to deal with complexity. We can make better decisions and have more productive conversations if we stay away from common mistakes and take the time to think critically about arguments.

In the end, the best way to resist emotional appeals is to keep a healthy level of skepticism and critical thinking. We should always ask ourselves if the arguments being made are based on facts and logic or if they are just trying to make us feel bad. By getting better at critical thinking, we can make it harder for people to play on our emotions and make better decisions based on reason and evidence.

Questions

1. How might you distinguish between a fallacy and a valid argument? What features or criteria would you use to make this determination?
2. In what ways might fallacies be used strategically or manipulatively in public discourse, and how can individuals protect themselves from being misled or deceived by these tactics?
3. Consider a recent news article or social media post that contains an example of a fallacy. How might you respond to this piece in a way that critiques the use of the fallacy while also engaging with the underlying argument or issue?
4. Some fallacies, like the straw man fallacy, rely on misrepresenting an opposing argument or position. In what ways might a person attempt to guard against being misrepresented, and how can they clarify their position to prevent this from happening?
5. Consider a real-world example of a fallacy that you have encountered (such as an ad hominem attack or an appeal to authority). How might you use critical thinking and evidence-based reasoning to evaluate the validity of the argument being presented, despite the presence of the fallacy?

PART FOUR

Overcoming
Cognitive Biases

X

Chapter 10: Identifying and Avoiding Common Biases that Lead to Poor Decision-Making

"The eye sees only what the mind is prepared to comprehend."

—ROBERTSON DAVIES

Cognitive biases are patterns of thinking that cause us to think in ways that are not logical or rational. They are a natural part of human psychology, but they can lead to poor decision-making and can prevent us from making the best choices. In this chapter, we'll look at some common cognitive biases that can make it hard to make good decisions, as well as ways to spot and get rid of them.

Confirmation Bias

Confirmation bias is the tendency to look for and understand information in a way that supports the beliefs and hypotheses we already have, instead of looking at all the evidence objectively. This bias can make us make bad decisions because it makes us ignore or downplay information that goes against what we already believe. To avoid confirmation bias, it's important to actively look for and think about evidence that might go against our beliefs. It's also important to keep an open mind and be willing to change our beliefs as new evidence comes in.

Sunk cost fallacy

Sunk cost fallacy is the tendency to keep putting time, money, or effort into a situation or decision, even if it's not in our best interests, because we've already put in those things. This bias can make us make bad decisions because it makes us stick with a bad choice instead of giving up and moving on. To avoid the sunk cost fallacy, it's important to focus on the potential future returns instead of the resources that have already been spent, and to be willing to walk away from a bad decision.

Availability Heuristic

The "availability heuristic" is the tendency to give more weight to events that are easy to remember or come to mind quickly. This bias can make it hard to make good decisions because it makes us overestimate the chances of rare or unlikely things happening and underestimate the chances of more common or likely things happening. To get around the availability heuristic, you need to look for a lot of different kinds of information and think about the base rate or the overall chance of something happening.

There are many other cognitive biases that can affect decision-making, such as the Halo effect, Anchoring, the framing effect, etc., but the ways to overcome them are the same as the ones above, which is to be aware of the biases you may have.

Here are some examples that illustrate the impact of cognitive biases on decision-making in the context of young adults and professionals:

1. Confirmation bias: A young adult is studying for a test in a subject they struggle with, they keep looking for examples, practice problems and explanations that confirms their understanding of the concept, thus ignoring or downplaying information that contradicts their understanding, they keep missing some aspects of the subject and may perform poorly on the test. A professional in an organization may ignore negative feedback from customers or colleagues and may only focus on the positive aspects of the product or service, the result may be a product or service that does not meet the customers' needs.

2. Sunk cost fallacy: A young adult has invested a lot of time and effort into a relationship that is not working out, but they feel reluctant to end it because of all the time and effort they've already invested, as a result, they end up in a unhealthy relationship for a longer period of time. A professional might invest in a project that is not feasible or profitable, but because of the resources already invested, they continue to invest more in it, this might lead to financial losses or missed opportunities.

3. Availability heuristic: A young adult might overestimate the probability of winning the lottery because they see lots of people winning and hear about it frequently in the news, they might believe that it's more likely to win the lottery than it actually is, and as a result, they may end up spending more money than they can afford on lottery tickets. A professional might overestimate the probability of a catastrophic event happening in their industry because of recent high-profile cases, they might take excessive measures to protect against this event, even though it might not be the best use of their resources.

Poor Decision-making Scenario

A young professional is working on a project that is falling behind schedule and over budget. They are under pressure from their manager to complete the project quickly, but they are also aware that they are running low on resources. They have invested a lot of time and money in the project, and they don't want to see their work go to waste. They become increasingly focused on trying to complete the project, even though it's clear that it's not going to be successful. They start to ignore negative feedback from team members and ignore the red flags that the project is going wrong. They fall prey to the sunk cost fallacy and the confirmation bias. They continue to pour resources into the project, even though it's clearly not going to be successful. This leads to more delays, more cost overruns, and eventually, the project is canceled, resulting in a significant financial loss. Here is an example of a good decision-making scenario where cognitive biases are being overcome:

Good Decision-making Scenario:

A young professional is working on a project that is falling behind schedule and over budget. They are under pressure from their manager to complete the project quickly, but they are also aware that they are running low on resources. They have invested a lot of time and money in the project, and they don't want to see their work go to waste. However, they recognize that their project is not going well, and they start to seek out diverse perspectives from their team members. They also start to look at the data and the evidence objectively, questioning their own assumptions and beliefs about the project. They are aware of the sunk cost fallacy and confirmation bias and actively work to over-come them. They make the difficult but necessary decision to cut their losses, and they walk away from the project before it causes further financial losses.

In this scenario, the young professional was able to make a difficult decision because they were aware of the potential for cognitive biases to affect their decision-making and actively worked to overcome them. They recognized that the sunk cost fallacy and confirmation bias were influencing their thinking, and they actively sought out diverse perspectives and information in order to make a more informed decision. They were able to objectively evaluate the data and evidence and make a decision that was in the best interest of the organization, rather than allowing themselves to be swayed by their own biases or the time and resources already invested in the project.

By taking this approach, the young professional was able to avoid further delays and cost overruns, and they saved the organization from a significant financial loss. Additionally, by cutting their losses and walking away from the project, they freed up resources and time that could be invested in more promising opportunities. They made a good decision, not only from a financial standpoint but also from the perspective of being able to make a decision that aligns with the organization's overall goals and priorities.

The above examples show the importance of being aware of cognitive biases, and how they can affect the decision-making process. These examples also show that by being aware of these cognitive biases, and by developing strategies to overcome them, one can make better decisions, and these decisions can have a positive impact on one's life, both personally and professionally.

By being aware of these cognitive biases, you can learn to recognize when they might be affecting their thoughts and behaviors. This awareness is an important first step in getting rid of these biases because it helps people be aware of how cognitive biases might affect their decisions. Furthermore, actively working to get rid of cognitive biases means coming up with ways to counteract what they do. Some of these strategies are looking for different points of view and information, questioning one's own assumptions and beliefs, and being willing to change one's mind when new evidence comes along.

It's also important to remember that cognitive biases are a normal part of human psychology and that we all have them to some degree. They are not a sign of weakness or not being smart, but a normal part of how people think. But just because cognitive biases are natural doesn't mean we should just let them affect our thinking. By working to overcome them, people can make better decisions and live more meaningful lives. You can reach your goals, solve problems, and make choices that fit with your values and priorities if you make better decisions.

Also, overcoming cognitive biases in your professional life can be especially helpful because it can help you make better decisions, solve problems better, communicate better, and use your time and resources more efficiently. Overall, if you are committed to becoming a better critical thinker and decision maker, regardless of your age or profession, you should be aware of cognitive biases and work to get rid of them.

Questions

1. Write an example of a time you fell prey to the sunk cost fallacy. What strategies can you use to avoid it the next time this may occur?
2. Can you think of a time when you have ignored information that contradicted your beliefs? How can you actively seek out and consider evidence that may contradict your beliefs?
3. Have you ever overestimated the probability of a rare event happening to you? How can you seek out a wide range of information and consider the base rate of an event to counteract the availability heuristic?
4. Are there any situations where you think you might have been influenced by confirmation bias? How can you actively seek out and consider alternative perspectives and information?
5. How do you think being aware of cognitive biases and actively working to overcome them can improve your decision-making and critical thinking abilities? How can you apply this knowledge in your personal and professional life?

XI

⚜

Chapter 11: An Analysis of Moral Values and Ethics

"Morality, like art, means drawing a line someplace."

-OSCAR WILDE

To properly grasp arguments and our own prejudices, we must first distinguish between morals and ethics. Morals and ethics are not the same thing, contrary to common opinion. They can and have clashed in a variety of ways throughout history. What exactly is moral? What exactly is ethics? These phrases have been carefully examined, argued about, and written about in great length throughout ancient history, from Socrates (339BC) in ancient Greece through Confucius (551 BC-479 BC) in ancient China. Before we look at why they can conflict in so many ways, I feel compelled to clarify the terms in their most fundamental form, without getting too philosophical.

Morals and ethics are defined differently depending on who you ask and where you look. In its most basic form, morals are defined as a concerned distinction of principles for what is good and bad, positive and negative, holy and evil, right and improper. Having good morals means being considered a righteous good person by the community of people who share your principles. Morals' derives from the Latin word "Mos," which signifies custom (habits). It is ruled by social and cultural standards. Several stories, depending on the culture, teach us moral lessons. Just think of children's books that provide lessons like "slow and steady wins the race" and "don't judge a book by its cover". These lessons are taught in western countries to influence young minds to do things like "take your time" and "get to know someone beyond looks". What about moral societies in general? Someone who is moral is someone who believes in equality for all, regardless of race, creed, or background. But, this moral individual may appear immoral if the other group believes in equity for everyone above equality because equity appears to be more justifiable in their eyes. We may say the same thing about religion; someone who follows the Qur'an, the Holy Bible, or the Hebrew Bible may appear moral to the religious community with which they are involved. However, an atheist or a religious organization other than the other may regard that group as immoral. In other words, morals are defined by who defines them and what THEIR morals are.

When it comes to definition, ethics is related to morals, but far more complex. Although ethics can be defined by who defines it, the individual possesses more truth than the group. Ethics is the process through which one holds oneself accountable. To put it another way, ethics can be more customized than morals. Ethics derives from the Greek term "Ethikos," which means "character," and is thus a reaction to a specific individual or event. Integrity, which falls under ethics, is one example of this. "Integrity is doing what is right when no one is looking," I tell my middle school students. But what is correct? What is right? This can be related to moral principles, and I could write an entire book on moral philosophy and ethics, but I digress. You, the reader, must respond to these questions. In reality, as perilous as this may sound, there is no correct or incorrect answer. But, if you need an example of what is right and just, consider this: Can you perform the deed and then look in the mirror, smile, and be happy of yourself without acknowledging others?

When we favor particular morality over ethical behaviors, a conflict occurs. Worse, this generally results in the deaths or subjugation of other people's organizations. The annihilation of the Jewish population was a moral value in Nazi Germany. What was the importance of these morals? As the war drew to a close, the Allies evacuated troops to the concentration camps and attempted to hasten the execution of their inmates rather than bolstering their combat force. Consider that for a moment. If you were in command of an army, would you rather try to win the war or destroy a certain group of noncombatants? Your moral compass will be determined by your response. Additionally, morality might change over time or become immoral by the next community leader. This is one of the risks of Moral Policing.

In the past, moral policing was usually initiated by religion. Many people believe it started with the Spanish Inquisition, but they are inaccurate. Moral policing is any sort of regulation based on morals. According to historians[14], including the Muslim community, the crucifixion of Jesus Christ (and anyone who refuted specific doctrines within the Jewish religion at the time) was an actual procedure, and Jesus Christ was an actual person. It is said in the book of Matthew within the Christian Holy Bible that the Jewish community was given the option of releasing a guilty murder and punishing Jesus or letting Jesus go and crucifixion the convicted killer. During the Mihna period of Islamic history, 'Abbasid Caliph al-Ma'mun imposed punishment, jail, or death on religious experts who did not adhere to Mutazila doctrine (a specific ideology or denomination within the Muslim religion)[15]. Then there was the Spanish Inquisition, which was carried out by the Catholic church and resulted in the murder of around 32,000 people, while historians argue that the number could be far higher.

Yet, this type of moral police is merely a modest illustration of moral policing's global history. It did not take long for the Americas to establish systems of moral policing within the colonies and, later, across the states. The Salem Witch Trials are an example of moral policing in American history. Puritans (commonly mistaken for pilgrims) initiated a series of witch trials in 1692 in response to reports of immoral behavior. Historians believe the first immoral conduct began with two young girls (historians suggest an 11-year old and a 9-year old). They were diagnosed with bewitchment by the doctor. There has also been record of adulterous affairs involving widows or young married women with Puritan leaders. It was then extended to include women who rebuffed sexual advances from other Puritan men, as well as allegations from envious married women. The moral value of the Puritans, as well as the accusation of witchcraft and devil worship, gave judges more power than citizens. It was also useful to know that individuals who were accused and executed lost their land, while the leaders were free to redistribute it as they saw fit.

This extreme type of moral policing required no evidence, only allegation. There was no opportunity for repentance or due process; you were just guilty unless proven innocent. If the accused declared their innocence, they would be tied up and thrown into a lake, where if they drowned, they were innocent, and if they floated up, they were guilty. This practice was discontinued after only one year, yet twenty-five persons were slain in the name of the Salem Witch Trials. Moral policing persisted, with victims ranging from former slaves to religious groups (regardless of skin color). The founders of the United States founded its constitution on aspects of a just republic and morality based on Judeo-Christian views of justice, freedom, individualism, and equality.

Yet, within critical theory ideology, we observe a new sort of moral policing in the twenty-first century. If you speak out against a certain organization or concept, you will be scolded and "canceled," which usually entails getting fired from a job that has nothing to do with the issue and being denied essential services that you may require to survive. In other words, your life is "canceled". One could argue that this is more humane than crucifixion, forced re-education, an iron maiden, or drowning, but is this the decision you desire for everybody who disagrees with you? If history has any sense of recurrence or rhyme, no moral standing lasts and the pendulum inevitably swings the other way. And if you agree with moral policing, what innocence will you profess the next time you're nailed to a cross or see the shackles that will bound you by the lake? What does this have to do with critical thinking? Surprisingly, quite a bit.

Regardless of the information you discover, the conclusion, judgment, or results must be ethical and honest, even if it goes against your own moral beliefs. If you disagree with a result, if you dismiss or ignore your findings because they do not fit your morals, you have failed science and critical thinking. It's as straightforward and cruel as that. This is something that many social scientists do. If the study does not meet their moral standards, many of them scrap the study or worse, remove conflicting premises and facts such that the conclusion fits their moral judgements. Because it gathers information before making a decision, critical thinking avoids the possibility of moral policing. Guilty until proven innocent is not a critical thinker because it contradicts the logical thinker's very character. Prior to making a decision, we must ensure that the premises are truthful, factual, and relevant. It is not sound logic to conclude that all men cheat because John is a guy and he cheated. Religion, ideology, sexual orientation, race, and moral convictions are all examples of this. In other words, remember your ethics regardless of your history or moral convictions.

Morals deal with the ideals of what is "right" and "wrong" whereas Ethics deals with what is "good" and what is "evil". They should both be aligned. It is crucial to be able to look in the mirror, smile, and be pleased with what you feel is good and right without any outside acknowledgement. But if you require reinforcement from someone else, you may need to reconsider your ethics and principles.

Questions

1. **Reflect on Morals and Ethics:** Examine your own moral values; Think about your ideas of how others should be treated, your work habits, and your ideas of what makes a strong minded human. Is it a positive force that your loved ones may benefit from? How about strangers? If it is positive, are you following those values? If not, why not?
    ◦ Write down a list of your moral and ethical values and highlight the ones that follow on a daily basis. Now look at the ones that may not be highlighted and begin to think of ideas on what you can do to live by those goals.
2. **Question:** Examine a moral policing situation that was actually a positive one for you. What elements of this did you find morally good? How did you think the opposition felt? Why did they feel strongly against the policy?
    ◦ **TIP:** DO NOT demonize the opposing element. Find actual evidence to support their arguments. Look for the logical premises if there are any.
3. **Small Project-Based Practice:** Define your morals/ethics and find a historical figure outside of your country and race. Examine their values and how they compare and contrast with yours. Now find a historical figure with the opposite views (simple online search of anything that is the opposite of your values). Examine their values and do a compare and contrast. Was there any moral policing from those historical figures? If so, what was the outcome?
    ◦ **NOTE:** The idea of this exercise is to analyze people who may not have any connections to you but may share the same moral and ethical values. Furthermore, it is necessary to be cautious about oppressing those whose values differ from your own.

PART FIVE

Critical Thinking in Action

XII

❦

Chapter 12: Critical Thinking in Different Areas of Life

"A mind all logic is like a knife all blade. It makes the hand bleed that uses it."

—RABINDRANATH TAGORE

The ability to think critically is a vital skill that can be put to use in a variety of contexts throughout one's life. In this chapter, we will investigate the various applications of critical thinking throughout history, as well as contemporary applications in fields such as politics, science, the media, and personal relationships, with the goal of enhancing the caliber of communication and decision-making in these spheres.

Critical Thinking in Politics

Throughout history, it has been important to be able to think critically in order to critically assess the claims made by political leaders and the positions they take on issues. During the Age of Enlightenment, for example, thinkers like Voltaire and Rousseau used critical thinking to criticize the idea that kings have divine right to rule and the idea that they have absolute power. During that time, this led to the development of democratic ideas and institutions. In today's world, you need to be able to think critically in order to judge the arguments and positions of political leaders and candidates. It is important to be able to recognize arguments and judge them for their validity. It is also important to be able to think about different points of view. By improving our critical thinking skills, we will not only be able to spot and fight against propaganda and manipulation, but we will also be able to choose political candidates and policies with more knowledge.

This means looking at political leaders' and candidates' plans, speeches, and actions to see if they make sense, are backed up by evidence, and are in line with the Constitution, ethical principles, or the common good. This also means being aware of possible biases, conflicts of interest, and hidden ambitions. An examination of political discourse, debates, and coverage in the media, with the goal of uncovering logical fallacies, claims that are misleading, and propaganda: This means learning how to spot common logical fallacies like the Strawman fallacy, the slippery slope, and the ad-hominem attack, as well as how to spot the use of emotional language, the manipulation of images, and the spreading of false information.

Consider other points of view on political issues. This means being willing to listen to and learn from different points of view, doing research on different points of view, and being able to explain why different positions are right or wrong. This gives people a more complete picture of the issues and helps them make better decisions. Identifying logical errors and biases in political talk: This means being aware of common cognitive biases like Confirmation bias and the sunk cost fallacy and recognizing when these biases might be affecting one's own thinking or the thinking of others. This can help people avoid making decisions that aren't good for them or for society as a whole.

Critical Thinking in Science

Science theories and discoveries have been made with the help of critical thinking throughout history. Galileo Galilei, for example, used critical thinking to evaluate the Aristotelian view of the universe that was popular at the time and come up with the heliocentric model of the solar system. Today, you need to be able to think critically in order to evaluate scientific research and theories. By using critical thinking skills, we can check the validity of scientific arguments and theories and find and get rid of cognitive biases that can mess up scientific thinking. Also, we can use critical thinking to judge how the news reports on scientific discoveries, which can help us avoid sensationalized or false information.

Putting scientific research and theories to the test: This means looking at the research methods, data, sample size, and conclusions of scientific studies to see if they are valid, reliable, and able to be repeated. Also being looked at is how well the theories fit with the available data, how well they are backed up by evidence, and if the research answers an important question.

Analysis of scientific evidence and data to find mistakes or biases: This means looking for possible sources of bias in the research design, like researcher bias or selection bias, and being aware of the study's limitations, looking for differences in the data, and judging how strong the conclusions are.

Look for different points of view on scientific issues: This means being willing to look at different theories and hypotheses, research from different fields and institutions, and voices in the scientific community that disagree with you. This can help you understand the issue from more than one point of view and weigh the evidence more carefully.

Identifying mistakes in reasoning and biases in scientific thinking:

This means being aware of common cognitive biases like the availability heuristic and the hindsight bias and recognizing when these biases might be affecting one's own thinking or the thinking of others. Also, be aware of common logical fallacies like the appeal to authority, which is when someone uses the approval of an authority to prove that a claim is true.

Critical Thinking in Media

Critical thinking has always been important for figuring out how to use the information we're given. In this age of information, when there is so much information available, it's important to be able to tell which sources are reliable and how strong an argument is. Today, we need to be able to think critically in order to evaluate the information we get from traditional media or social media. This helps us spot propaganda and false information. Critical thinking can also be used to judge how the news reports on events and issues, which can help us avoid getting biased or false information.

Assessing the reliability of sources and the validity of arguments in news stories and social media posts: This means finding reliable sources and judging whether the information given is correct and complete. This also means being aware of the authors, publishers, or platforms' possible biases, conflicts of interest, and hidden goals.

Identification of biases and misleading information in news coverage: This means being aware of common cognitive biases like the Anchoring bias and the Halo effect, which can change how people think about information, and recognizing when these biases might be affecting one's own thinking or the thinking of others. Also, be aware of misleading information like clickbait headlines and sensationalist language, which are ways to get people's attention and make them feel something.

Seeking out different points of view and information sources to get a more complete picture of an event. This means looking at more than one source of information about an event or issue to get a fuller picture. This can include things like reading news from different countries and cultures and listening to different points of view.

How to spot logical errors and propaganda techniques in the media: This means being aware of common mistakes in reasoning, like the bandwagon fallacy, and being able to tell when these mistakes are affecting your own thinking or the thinking of others. Also, you should know about propaganda techniques like loaded language, appealing to emotions, and transfer, which are used to make people like an idea or group. By recognizing and understanding these tactics, you can avoid being manipulated and make better decisions.

Critical Thinking in Personal Relationships

Critical thinking is vital in personal relationships because it helps you evaluate the arguments and points of view of others and make good decisions. We can evaluate the arguments of our friends and family by using critical thinking skills. We can also find and let go of cognitive biases that can affect our thinking in personal relationships. For example, using critical thinking can help you avoid confirmation bias and approach disagreements with an open mind, which leads to more constructive and effective communication. Critical thinking can also be used to judge how families and friends share the news reports on events and issues. This helps us avoid getting biased or false information that could affect our personal relationships.

Taking into account the points of view and arguments of friends and family: This means thinking about the reasons, facts, and assumptions behind what people close to you say, ask, or tell you. This can help find any possible misunderstandings and make communication clearer.

Recognizing cognitive biases such as Confirmation bias, which can affect how people think about their relationships: This means being aware of the cognitive biases that can affect one's own thinking or the thinking of others and noticing when these biases might be affecting one's relationships. Confirmation bias is a common bias that can hurt personal relationships. It means that people interpret information in a way that supports their own beliefs and biases and ignore information that goes against them.

Seeking out different points of view and being willing to consider them in disagreements and discussions: This means being open to hearing other people's points of view, understanding their reasoning and evidence, and being willing to consider different points of view. This can help to resolve conflicts and build stronger relationships.

Identifying logical fallacies used in personal arguments: This means being aware of common logical fallacies like Strawman, Ad Hominem, and Tu Quoque, which can be used to misrepresent or hurt an argument or a person. Knowing when these fallacies are used can help you figure out when someone is trying to trick or manipulate you and give you a better idea of how to respond.

By using critical thinking skills in different parts of our lives, we can improve the way we talk to each other and make decisions. We can make better decisions and avoid falling for cognitive biases if we know more about them. Critical thinking has been important throughout history, and it is still important in places like politics, science, the media, and personal relationships.

But it's important to remember that critical thinking is a skill that needs to be developed and used over and over again. It takes time and work to develop the process. People can improve their ability to think critically and make better decisions by doing it over and over again and being aware of cognitive biases.

As a final note, the examples above are not all there is to know about critical thinking. It can be used in many areas of life, not just the ones listed above. And by using critical thinking in different parts of life, a person can make their life more meaningful and satisfying.

Questions

1. Recall: Define and create an example of Strawman, Ad Hominem, and Tu Quoque
2. How do these examples relate to the critical thinking skills you have learned throughout this book?
3. How can you apply these examples to other areas of your life?
4. How can you use these examples to improve your critical thinking in your everyday life?
5. How can you apply these examples in the context of your personal and professional goals?

XIII

Chapter 13: Critical thinking and Creativity

"Logic will get you from A to B. Imagination will take you everywhere."

—ALBERT EINSTEIN

Both in one's personal life and in one's professional life, one needs to be successful in a number of different areas, including creativity and the capacity to think critically. Creativity helps people come up with fresh and unique ideas, while critical thinking enables them to analyze and assess the material they encounter, which in turn enables them to come to sound conclusions. When these two skills are combined, the result might be the creation of solutions that are not only innovative but also practical.

If you take a look at the various steps that go into the creative process, you may have a better understanding of the connection between critical thinking and creative thinking. The initial step is to come up with ideas for the project. People think in a variety of ways here, which results in a large number of unique ideas being generated. The suggestions will then be evaluated in the second step. Convergent thinking is utilized at this point so that individuals can assess and prioritize the ideas that they have generated. Putting the idea into practice is the third and last phase in the process. When it comes to planning, organizing, and carrying out the idea, here is where people apply their analytical thinking.

Idea Generation Stage:

1. At this stage, people use divergent thinking to come up with a lot of different ideas. Divergent thinking is the ability to come up with an extensive range of varying ideas and possibilities. It's a way to let your mind wander, think outside the box, and come up with new and different ideas. A brainstorming session, where a group of people get together to come up with lots of ideas for a new marketing campaign, is an example of this stage. The goal is to come up with as many ideas as possible without being overly critical of them.

Idea Evaluation Stage:

2. At this stage, people use convergent thinking to evaluate and rank the ideas they've come up with. Convergent thinking is being able to compare and rank ideas so that you can choose the best one. For example, after the brainstorming session, your marketing team or any trusted people in your inner circle can help you analyze the ideas that came up and figure out which ones are most likely to work, will have the most value, and/or will appeal to the target audience the most. The group (or you) then picks the idea that seems to have the most potential and works on it further. Critical thinking strategies will be more crucial than ever if you are working on an idea by yourself. Because of this, it's important to talk about and think about this with other people. You can (and should) participate in a number of social groups that may already be working on similar ideas. Use the ideas of

other people so that you can make a better decision.
Implementation Stage:

3. In this step, people plan, organize, and carry out the chosen idea by using critical thinking. At this stage, you need to be able to think critically to make sure that the idea can be put into action. As an example of this stage, once your group's idea has been chosen, the team plans, organizes, and runs the campaign, making sure it's done well, quickly, and efficiently.

Let's examine a few scenarios:

Scenario 1: The Business Owner/Manager

Idea Generation Stage:

1. A small business owner wants to grow her business and find new ways to make money. She sets aside time for a meeting with her team to talk about ideas. During the session, they come up with many different ideas, such as making a new line of products, adding more services, or moving into a new market. The goal is to come up with as many ideas as possible without judging them too much.
Idea Evaluation Stage:

2. After the brainstorming session, the team looks at all the ideas and decides which ones are most likely to work, won't cost too much, and will appeal to the target audience the most. They also think about how each idea fits in with the business's overall goals and objectives. In this case, the team chooses the most promising idea, which is making a new product line, and immediately begins working on it.
Implementation Stage:

3. The team then uses critical thinking to plan, organize, and carry out the chosen idea, which in this case is the development of a new product line. They do research on the market to find out

what their target audience needs and what features the product should have. They also come up with a plan for manufacturing, selling, and advertising the new product. The team also keeps an eye on how the new product line is doing and makes any changes that are needed to make sure it does well.

In this scenario, the small business owner uses both critical thinking and creativity throughout the creative process. In the first stage, he or she comes up with a lot of ideas. In the second stage, he or she evaluates the ideas and picks the best one. In the final stage, the chosen idea is put into action in an efficient and effective way.

Scenario 2: The Teacher

Idea Generation Stage:

1. A high school teacher wants to come up with a new way to teach a tough subject, like math. He makes time for a brainstorming session with his coworkers to come up with an assortment of different ways to teach the subject. During the session, they come up with strategies for making the material more interesting for students, like using real-life examples, incorporating technology, and doing hands-on activities. The goal is to come up with as many ideas as possible without judging them too much.
   Idea Evaluation Stage:
2. After the brainstorming session, the teacher decides which ideas are most likely to work, which will bare minimum cost, and which her students will be most interested in. She also thinks about how each idea fits with the class's lesson plan and learning goals. The teacher decides that the most effective way to teach is to use examples from real life and technology.
   Implementation Stage:
3. The teacher then uses critical thinking to plan, organize, and carry out the chosen idea, which in this case is to teach with

real-life examples and technology. He comes up with lesson plans that include interactive activities and homework that show how math is used in the real world. He also looks for things like videos, interactive simulations, and apps that can help the student understand the material better. He also keeps an eye on how his students are doing and makes changes to his teaching style as needed.

In this scenario, the instructor makes use of both critical thinking and creative thinking throughout the entire process of creating something new. From the beginning of the process, he thinks of many different ways to instruct. At the second stage, he analyzes the suggestions and decides which one is the most promising. At the final stage, he puts the most promising idea into action in a manner that is both productive and fruitful. Because of this, his students will have a better understanding of the content and a higher level of interest in the process of studying it.

Scenario 3: The Parent(s)

Idea Generation Stage:

1. When a parent wants their child to be more active and receive more exercise, they look for new ways to encourage those behaviors in their child. They scheduled a time to get together with other parents and discuss the best ways to encourage their children to participate in more active pursuits. During the course of the discussion, they come up with suggestions such as signing up for a sports team, going on walks as a family, and trying out new activities such as rock climbing or dancing. The objective is to generate as many ideas as possible without placing too much emphasis on evaluating them.
Idea Evaluation Stage:
2. After the brainstorming session, the parent will assess the several

ideas to determine which ones are the most practicable, have the most value, and will appeal to her child the most. They also take into consideration how well each concept fits in with the child's abilities and interests. Because the child has shown an interest in playing soccer, the parent concludes that it would be in the child's best interest to join a soccer team.

Implementation Stage:

3. The parent then applies analytical thought to the process of planning, organizing, and carrying out the selected plan, which in this example involves assisting the child in joining a sports team. She does research on the various soccer teams in the region and assesses which one would be the most suitable for her child by taking into consideration the level of skill, the coaching style, and the schedule of each team. In addition to this, she ensures that the child is adequately prepared for the tryouts, that the necessary equipment is purchased, and that transportation arrangements are made. In addition to this, the parent will continue to watch the child's development and will make any required modifications if the youngster requires them.

In this scenario, the parent utilizes both critical thinking and creative thinking throughout the entire creative process. In the first stage of the process, the parent comes up with a wide variety of ideas for getting her child to be more active. In the second stage, the parent evaluates the ideas and chooses the one that seems to have the most potential. Finally, in the third stage, the parent puts the idea that was chosen into action in an efficient and effective manner. As a consequence of this, the youngster participates in more active pursuits and is able to reap the benefits, both in terms of their physical health and their ability to interact with others, of joining a sports team.

If you want to apply divergent and convergent thinking in your day-to-day activities, you should strive to make time in your schedule for both the development of ideas and the evaluation of those ideas.

For instance, schedule some time to think about fresh concepts for a project you're currently working on, and then schedule some additional time in the future to assess which concepts hold the greatest promise. In addition, you should make an effort to expose yourself to new concepts and points of view, as this can assist in the generation of fresh and original ideas.

The stages of idea generation, evaluation, and implementation work together to help combine critical thinking and creativity. This is accomplished through the provision of a structured process for the generation of new ideas, followed by the evaluation of those ideas and the implementation of the idea that is determined to be the most successful. Individuals can ensure that they are creating a wide variety of ideas by going through these steps, and then analyzing their options and putting into action the most promising one by doing so.

Try to approach the process of idea creation with an open mind and a willingness to consider all of the options. This will help you practice idea generation without being critical of your own ideas. In addition, when you are in the stage of coming up with ideas, you should try not to concentrate too much on whether or not the ideas will be feasible, but rather on coming up with as many ideas as you possibly can. It is usually beneficial to have a variety of ideas at one's disposal for subsequent evaluation.

In order to apply critical thinking to the stage of the creative process known as implementation, it is essential to plan, organize, and carry out one's selected concept in a manner that is timely and effective. This entails recognizing and responding to any potential problems or roadblocks, as well as formulating a strategy to get over them. In addition to this, it is essential to monitor the development of the implementation in order to make any necessary modifications at the appropriate time.

While I was working on a project to revamp a website, for instance,

I used both critical thinking and creative thinking in my work. This is one example of how I've mixed the two. I came up with a wide variety of concepts through engaging in divergent thinking, which included a variety of possibilities for the layout and features. After that, I utilized convergent thinking to examine the various concepts and determine which ones were the most realistic and appealing to the audience in question. This included the use of color psychology, a study on how colors affect human moods and behaviors. In conclusion, I used analytical thinking to plan and carry out the redesign, ensuring that the newly redesigned website was both user-friendly and aesthetically pleasing, as well as that it achieved the goals of the project.

The ability to combine critical thinking with creative thinking is an important skill that can lead to the development of solutions that are both truly original and effective. The capacity of individuals can be improved by regularly exposing themselves to new ideas and experiences, as well as by actively engaging in both divergent and convergent thinking, establishing connections and seeing patterns, and making connections and seeing patterns.

Questions

1. How can you apply the use of different ways of thinking in your daily life?
2. How does the idea generation, evaluation and implementation stages help combine critical thinking and creativity?
3. How can you practice idea generation without being critical of your ideas?
4. How can you apply critical thinking to the implementation stage of the creative process?
5. Can you give an example of how you've combined critical thinking and creativity to generate an innovative idea?

XIV

❦

Chapter 14: Critical Thinking for your personal life

"Knowing is not enough; we must apply. Being willing is not enough; we must do."

—LEONARDO DE VINCI

Your odds of successfully forecasting what will take place in the future are quite poor if you do not have access to a time stone that can help you glimpse into the future. On the other hand, being able to forecast events by looking at the chance of those outcomes occurring is made possible via the practice of critical thinking, which is both an art and a science. You will not be correct each and every time, but there is a chance that you will be correct the majority of the time, or at the absolute least, you will have a forecast that is close enough to allow you to plan for the various outcomes that are possible. This situation is comparable to that of a poker player who determines how much money to wager depending on what he observes on the cards and how he interprets the behavior of the other players at the table. In point of fact, critical thinking may appear to be a hard subject if you are only considering it from an external standpoint or are inexperienced with the nuances of how to perform it; yet, the application of critical thinking in day-to-day life is not only basic but also useful. In spite of this, in order to become proficient at it, you are going to need to put in some practice and get familiar with the fundamentals. This particular instance makes reference to the parameters that govern existence. Let's imagine you're considering making an investment in the stock market or buying a house. Both of these are significant life decisions. You become aware of an opportunity that is simply too appealing for you to pass up on.

If you decide to go with this option, there is a possibility that your life may improve. In spite of this, you find that you are beginning to have second thoughts, and there may even be some wavering on your part. You almost get the sensation that someone is telling you not to carry it out in a hushed voice, which would be contrary to what you should do. You come to the conclusion that it is time for you to move on with your life and make a choice that will affect not just you but also the people you care about the most. Since the property is a dud, the neighborhood is hazardous, or the stock market bubble burst, you have experienced a huge setback financially. This may be the result of the fact that the stock market bubble burst. If you do not have the required skills or information and instead choose to rely exclusively on your gut feeling, it is highly improbable that you will be successful. You can't rule out the possibility of good fortune. But if it can't be repeated, then it's just a matter of luck rather than anything else. In order to carry out an activity more than once, one needs to have a plan, understand the cause and effect of actions, perform research on the data provided, and have a way to get to the result that is sought.

To think critically means to investigate every facet of an issue from every conceivable vantage point. If you feel the need to explain or defend the activities you've taken, it's likely that you're trying to offer yourself an explanation for why you took those actions rather than letting the evidence speak for itself. If you feel the need to explain or defend the activities you've taken, it's likely that you're trying to offer yourself an explanation for why you took those actions. If you can just show the proof, then there is not much more that needs to be spoken on the issue. You will no longer be perceived by other people as being eager and ugly; rather, they will begin to consider you to be mature and intellectual. This has the ability to result in successful relationships, opportunities in one's work, and success in life as a whole. If you have decided to read this book, then you are capable of finishing the work that needs to be done. It is important to stress this point since it is crucial.

It's unfortunate to add that I can't say the same about a lot of other people, but that's just the way it is. They also cannot be held responsible for it in any way. We are able to have feelings because of the way that we are constructed as individuals. Our physiological and mental necessities are the fundamental forces that influence our conduct. According to the "Hierarchy of Needs," which was devised by an American psychologist by the name of Abraham Harold Maslow, in order for humans to develop further, certain wants need to be addressed, at the very least partially[16]. The most essential physiological needs including food, water, warmth, and rest, are at the bottom of this hierarchy, which is more commonly depicted as a pyramid. This is the level that is most generally referred to as the "base." Once this objective has been achieved, the next most demanding fundamental requirements are going to be safety and security. After the physiologic needs of a human being have been satisfied, the individual's psychological needs will gradually come into focus. This begins with having a sense of belonging, which may be achieved through having intimate relationships as well as good friends. There are several occurrences of the Esteem below. The mental and emotional sensation of having accomplished something significant after having accomplished said something. At the very top of the hierarchy are the needs that are related with either self-actualization or self-fulfillment. Although the actualization of one's complete potential is not something

that happens to everyone over the course of their lives, it is something that everyone ought to have as their primary life objective. It is
my sincere wish that I can serve as a source of motivation for you on
your path toward self-actualization; however, in order to get there, you
will need to hone your analytical and deductive reasoning skills. It is
in your best interest to educate yourself, assess the circumstances you
find yourself in, and devise a strategy to address that predicament if
you find yourself in a precarious position as a result of a lack of safety
and security. If you find yourself in such a position, it is in your best
interest to educate yourself.

To put it another way, if the needs at the bottom of your hierarchy
of requirements aren't being satisfied, you need to engage in some serious problem-solving in order to figure out how to satisfy those wants
before you can proceed to the next level. In other words, you can't
move on to the next level until you've satisfied the needs at the bottom
of your hierarchy of requirements. The good news is that when one
advances in their career and rises up the organizational hierarchy, they
gain the ability to pause what they are doing and actively think for
longer periods of time. It is terrible that I have to admit that pausing to
think when you are fatigued, hungry, and cold is tremendously difficult
and requires a particular kind of inner fortitude that I can only attempt
to explain. Nonetheless, I will say that this is one of the most difficult
challenges I have ever faced. Critical thinking, on the other hand, not
only helps you in making crucial decisions, but it also has the potential
to supply answers to a great deal of the obstacles that you are now
facing. This is because critical thinking helps you examine problems
from multiple angles.

Imagine for a moment that you have a problem with a youngster
who is struggling academically in school. What action would you take?
You might go any one of many possible directions, including the following: You have the ability to compel yourself to feel emotions in order to
motivate yourself to put in more effort in order to attain higher levels

of success. You might try to empathize with their emotional needs and make an effort to connect with their natural feelings by demonstrating that you care about them. This could be accomplished by showing that you are concerned about them. You also have the option of conducting a full study of the problem, taking into account both the external and internal pressures that have been exerted on your child, and then coming up with a plan that will re-engage the child in order to get the desired result. In point of fact, there is no conclusive answer that can be pinned down as definitively pointing in the direction of the latter. Each and every child is one of a kind, just as each and every set of circumstances is one of a kind. A person who is competent in critical thinking has the ability to adapt, analyze, and come up with a strategy for any situation that they might find themselves in.

While looking for someone to share a home with, this principle should also be kept in mind. Wishes are something that all humans have, and as shown by Maslow's Hierarchy of Needs, these wants can be satisfied in a variety of ways depending on the individual. A quarrel may arise if one of the people living in the house with you has their heart set on pizza, while one of the people living in the house with you has one of their core wants to eat Asian cuisine. This very little argument has the potential to grow into a far more significant one if it is not resolved. Keeping one's feelings about various options out of the decision-making process is a crucial aspect of critical thinking, and thus ties in with that concept. Does it really make a difference if they choose the exact same thing to eat two days in a row or if their moral standards are diametrically opposed to yours? In order to accomplish this, you need to put aside your feelings and ask yourself, "Is this somebody that I can be happy with for the next fifty to one hundred years?" Do any of their behaviors irritate me to a very little degree, or do none of them at all? Is it even somewhat conceivable for me to respect the ethical standards that they uphold? It's possible that you'll have an overwhelming rush of warm and fuzzy emotions when you meet someone for the first time. In addition to that, they might have a charming sense of humor, an appealing figure, and a lovely smile. Is having a good time more important to you than meeting someone with whom you can create a life together? When you're in a mood where you don't feel like laughing, do you ever find that your sense of humor can be too much for you to handle? Would you still have the same gorgeous smile and enticing body in the next fifty to one hundred years? What if they were in an accident and they no longer had those features after the event?

But, in order to evaluate whether or not this requires you to participate in critical thinking about the circumstances, you will first need to do an analysis of the situation in order to determine what your goals are. If it is something that could have an effect on your future or the future of the people around you, such as your loved ones, your community, or your government, I cannot stress enough how important it is that you remove your emotions from the decision-making process and instead focus on analyzing the situation logically. If it is something that could have an effect on your future or the future of the people around you, I cannot stress enough how important it is that you remove your emotions from the decision-making process. If, on the other hand, you are only trying to pick where you want to hang out over the weekend, we hope that you will use some common sense in approaching the matter and that you will have a fantastic time regardless of the option that you make.

Critical thinking is, in the end, the defining characteristic that separates leaders from the masses. This manner of thinking was exhibited in some form or another by every notable figure who has ever lived throughout history. George Washington, for example, created an executive cabinet in order to gather different minds together so that he can get all the facts necessary to make a proper decision as President of the United States. And to be clear, I am not advising you to compare yourself to historical figures of the past. Rather, what I am advising you to do is compare yourself to the person you were the day before.

You need to perform some self-reflection on the decisions and choices you've made in your life, practice some humility, and figure out how to admit when you're wrong. In other words, you need to figure out how to admit when you're wrong. It is OK to make decisions based on one's feelings and to behave hastily every once in a while. It is NOT acceptable to justify your acts by making up excuses and refusing to learn from the consequences of those actions. It is also not acceptable to study this book, gain information from it, and then not put any of that knowledge into practice at all. This is not acceptable. That is the same as an artist who never exhibits their creations, a surgeon who only treats themselves, and a teacher who refuses to instruct a pupil who is willing to learn. Those that are capable of critical thinking are expected to share their knowledge and experience with others in order to encourage the growth of further critical thinkers. This is the kind of information that can be helpful not only to you but also to the people who are important to you, your community, and even your government if it is shared. The acquisition of skills that cannot be used by other people or shared is comparable to using the restroom, with the one and only difference being that once you are finished using the restroom, you are obligated to take the additional step of ensuring that the toilet is flushed. This is analogous to the acquisition of skills that cannot be used by other people or shared. If you want to have a prosperous future, you need to make the most of the abilities and skills you already possess, as well as concentrate on growing your understanding of those abilities and developing your critical thinking skills.

Play to Win

Like a poker player who evaluates their bet after analyzing the cards and the other players at the table, a person who is skilled in the art and science of critical thinking is able to determine outcomes based on probability. This is very similar to the situation in which a person who is skilled in the art and science of critical thinking is able to determine the Even while it might not be possible to know the future in its totality, using critical thinking can help in making educated guesses and preparing for various outcomes. On the other hand, critical thinking might appear to be difficult and intimidating, particularly for individuals who are unfamiliar with the notion. The most important thing is to get a grasp on the principles of critical thinking and use them in your day-to-day life.

When it comes to making significant choices in one's life, such as purchasing a home or putting money into the stock market, this is a good illustration of what I mean. There is a possibility that an opportunity will present itself that appears to be too excellent to pass up; nevertheless, hesitancy and uncertainty may occur. When choosing a choice, it is critical to take into account the facts and research that is currently available, comprehend the relationship between the causes and consequences of the various options, and formulate a strategy. One is able to come up with decisions that are well-informed and have a better chance of being successful if they think analytically and take into account the circumstance in its entirety.

It is also essential to keep in mind that critical thinking is more than just coming to the correct conclusions; it also requires one to be able to justify and clarify such conclusions. The ability to give evidence and rationale to back one's actions can lead to favorable relationships, opportunities in one's profession, and overall success.

Nonetheless, it is necessary to admit that critical thinking can be difficult, particularly for people who are not satisfying their fundamental physiological and psychological needs. This is especially true in the case of individuals who are in poverty. According to the Hierarchy of Needs, which was developed by the American psychologist Dr. Abraham Harold Maslow, in order for a person to advance to the next level of growth and self-actualization, they must first have all of their fundamental wants satisfied. For instance, if a person is having trouble obtaining food, water, warmth, or safety, it is important to use critical thinking to figure out how to meet those needs before focusing on self-actualization and thinking about more complex issues than basic necessities. This should be done before thinking about how to address more advanced problems.

It is also crucial to note that critical thinking can be difficult in adverse circumstances, such as when one is cold, hungry, or weary. This is something that should be kept in mind. It is only by self-discipline and consistent practice that one can acquire the ability to step back and actively think when faced with a circumstance like this.

In addition, critical thinking is a process that never ends and calls for continuous practice as well as continued education. It is essential to constantly test and question one's own views and assumptions, as well as to look for new facts and knowledge to add to one's repertoire. One's critical thinking skills, as well as their ability to forecast and prepare for various events, can continue to improve if they take this step.

Critical thinking is a crucial skill that can be improved with practice, and one of its benefits is the capacity to forecast outcomes and make judgments that are well-informed. It is possible to improve one's ability to foresee outcomes and make wise choices by dissecting information, examining patterns and connections, interpreting the relevance of information, assessing the trustworthiness and quality of sources, and drawing inferences. Critical thinking, on the other hand, should not be seen as a form of superstition but rather as a logical and systematic approach to evaluating information. It is important to remember that developing this skill takes time and practice, and that critical thinking should not be viewed as a form of superstition. In addition, it is essential to keep in mind that critical thinking has the potential to assist us not just in achieving self-actualization and self-fulfillment but also in satisfying our fundamental need, such as a feeling of safety and security. It is a useful instrument that can guide us through the intricacies of life and assist us in making better decisions that will lead to success in both our professional and personal lives.

Questions

1. Can you give an example of a time when you had to use critical thinking to solve a problem in your personal life?
2. How do you evaluate the credibility and reliability of information sources when making important decisions?
3. Can you explain a time when your initial assumptions about a situation were challenged, and how you adjusted your thinking accordingly?
4. When faced with conflicting viewpoints or information, how do you approach synthesizing and reconciling the different perspectives?
5. Can you give an example of a time when you had to analyze a problem from multiple perspectives before reaching a conclusion?

PART SIX

Critical Thinking in The Workplace

XV

Chapter 15: Critical thinking in the workplace

"When intuition and logic agree, you are always right."

—BLAISE PASCAL

The ability to think critically is one of the most important skills that one must possess in order to be successful in the modern workplace. It requires the capability to examine information, evaluate facts, and make conclusions that are rational and informed based on that evaluation. This ability is necessary for finding solutions to issues, determining what steps to take, and communicating successfully with other people. In this chapter, we will discuss the significance of critical thinking in the workplace, as well as provide some examples of how it can be applied to a variety of tasks, including the resolution of problems, the formation of sound decisions, and the establishment of clear lines of communication with other people.

The Importance of Critical Thinking in the Workplace

In the modern day's fast-paced corporate world, having a logical mind is absolutely necessary. It is a crucial talent that enables individuals to assess information, recognize issues, and think of solutions that are effective. The capacity to think critically can provide a worker with a considerable competitive edge over other workers since it enables them to make better judgments, find solutions to problems more quickly, and communicate with more clarity.

Critical thinking is an essential component in the process of decision-making, which is one of the most significant components of working in an organization. When it comes to making decisions, it is essential to assess the usefulness of the information at hand, consider the advantages and disadvantages of the many alternatives, and settle on the most appropriate action to take. Those who are able to think critically are able to assess the evidence at their disposal and come to judgments that are informed, which in turn increases the likelihood that those decisions will result in success.

Critical thinking is an essential component in a number of processes, including problem solving, which is another essential element of the working environment. When confronted with a problem, it is essential to determine the core cause of the issue rather than only treating the symptoms of the problem. Critical thinking enables people to recognize problems at their roots and come up with workable solutions that get to the root of the issue rather than just treating the symptoms.

Critical thinking is a crucial skill for achieving successful results in one's professional communications. When people are able to think about things in a more analytical manner, they are better able to explain their ideas and convey themselves clearly. They are also better able to listen to what is being said by others and comprehend the viewpoints of others. The ability to communicate effectively is critical for successful teamwork, collaboration, and the development of professional relationships.

Examples of Critical Thinking in the Workplace

Here are a few examples of how critical thinking can be applied in the workplace:

1. Problem-solving: A manufacturing firm detects a decrease in production speed. A critical thinker would collect information about the manufacturing procedure, studying factors like machine output and worker efficiency. To get to the bottom of things, they would also poll workers on the ground for their input. The critical thinker would next devise a strategy to boost the production rate, such as fine-tuning the equipment, re-arranging the workflow, or re-educating the workforce, once the underlying problem has been recognized.

2. Decision-making: The marketing team is debating whether to start a new advertising drive. The campaign's prospective costs and advantages would be weighed by a critical thinker, who would then base their judgment on the information at hand. They would take into account not only the company's aims and resources, but also the market and the competition. A critical thinker would also weigh the campaign's long-term effects on the company's reputation and brand against the risks involved.

3. Communication: A team leader is tasked with giving a presentation to the executive board of the organization. A person who is capable of critical thought will be able to articulate their thoughts clearly, respond to potential objections, and anticipate questions. They'd take into account the listeners' level of familiarity with the topic at hand, as well as their worldview and experience, and adjust their presentation accordingly. Before giving a presentation, a critical thinker would run through it in their head and ask for feedback.

Developing Critical Thinking Skills

Although some people may be born with innately high levels of critical thinking ability, it is a skill that can be honed and perfected with practice. If you want to sharpen your critical thinking abilities, try these strategies:

- Practice active listening: The ability to actively listen to what other people are saying while simultaneously being able to comprehend and evaluate what they are saying is a key component of critical thinking. When engaging in conversation with other people, it is important to pay attention to what they have to say and make an effort to comprehend the perspective from which they are speaking.
- Read widely: Reading a wide variety of texts will help you become more familiar with a variety of points of view and can contribute to the development of your analytical and deductive reasoning abilities.
- Take on new challenges: You can sharpen your analytical abilities by stretching your comfort zone and taking on new challenges. The best way to accomplish this is to take on additional duties at work or to initiate your own projects outside of work.
- Learn from others: Find people who have great critical thinking skills and learn from them. There are plenty of people out there. You can accomplish this goal by engaging in conversation with mentors or by taking part in events for professional growth.
- Reflect on your own thinking: Take time on a regular basis to reflect on the ways in which you think and challenge the assumptions you make about yourself. You should make an effort to comprehend how you arrived at a specific judgment or conclusion, and you should search for any biases that might have influenced your thinking.

Fostering a Culture of Critical Thinking

A critical thinking culture can be fostered within a company to help in the development of critical thinking skills in its population in addition to the individual's own efforts to improve their critical thinking abilities. One way to accomplish this is to:

- Creating an environment in which employees are encouraged to question and challenge assumptions
- Making available chances for continued education and professional growth.
- Fostering group effort and accepting a wide range of perspectives
- Developing a setting in which it is acceptable to take chances and experience failure.
- In the process of decision making and problem solving, recognizing and rewarding critical thinking is extremely beneficial.

The ability to think critically is one of the most important skills that one must possess in order to be successful in the modern workplace. It gives people the ability to assess information, recognize issues, and devise effective solutions. Individuals can improve their overall effectiveness and help contribute to the success of their organization by learning how to apply critical thinking to various tasks, such as problem-solving, decision-making, and communicating effectively with others. By understanding the significance of critical thinking and learning how to apply it to these tasks, individuals can contribute to the success of their organization. In addition, by cultivating a culture of critical thinking inside a company, leaders have the ability to assist their employees in the development of the skills they need to be successful, which eventually contributes to the success of the organization as a whole.

Questions

1. Think about a time when you had to make an important decision at work (or home). How did you use critical thinking in the process?
2. How do you approach problem-solving in the workplace? Are there any specific techniques you use to identify the root cause of a problem?
3. What are some of the challenges you have faced when communicating effectively with others in the workplace? How do you work to overcome these challenges?

XVI

꩜

Chapter 16: Fostering a Culture of Critical Thinking

"A people without the knowledge of their past history, origin, and culture is like a tree without roots."

—MARCUS GARVEY

It is necessary to cultivate a culture of critical thinking in the workplace if one wants to produce a labor force that is able to make decisions based on accurate information, efficiently solve problems, and communicate effectively. Organizations may assist their employees develop the abilities they need to be successful, which will eventually drive the success of the firm, if they encourage critical thinking among their workforce. In this chapter, we will discuss the benefits of encouraging critical thinking inside an organization as well as the different ways that this may be accomplished.

What is a culture of critical thinking?

A culture of critical thinking refers to the atmosphere that exists inside an organization and both values and supports the development of critical thinking abilities. It is defined by an openness to examine assumptions, evaluate evidence, and make conclusions that are rational and informed based on that evaluation. Teams are encouraged to think for themselves, voice their views, and question the existing quo in an environment that fosters critical thinking as a culture.

The numerous advantages that can result from cultivating a culture of critical thinking

There are a variety of positive outcomes that can result from cultivating a culture of critical thinking in the workplace. The most important of which are as follows:

- Improved decision-making: Organizations can foster a setting more conducive to data-driven decision making by fostering a culture that values critical thinking among its staff. A more likely outcome is that they will consider all of their options, gather all relevant information, and make an informed decision.
- Increased problem-solving capabilities: Workers who are encouraged and allowed to use their critical thinking skills are better able to identify problems and develop effective solutions. This has given me confidence that I can find solutions to issues more rapidly and efficiently.
- Improved communication: Facilitating employees' ability to think critically and express their thoughts articulately is a key benefit of fostering a critical thinking culture in the workplace. As a result, employees are better able to share information and work together to achieve organizational goals.
- Enhanced creativity and innovation: A culture of critical thinking can help firms develop an atmosphere in which employees are encouraged to think creatively and come up with new and unique ideas. This environment can be created by promoting a culture of critical thinking inside an organization.

- Better risk management: An organization with a culture of critical thinking is better able to assess the hazards posed by alternative courses of action and take precautions accordingly, ultimately resulting in reduced risk.

Creating a culture of critical thinking

Here are a few steps that organizations can take to foster a culture of critical thinking:

- Encourage employees to ask questions and challenge assumptions: Organizations can encourage a critical thinking culture by making it a place where employees are free to voice their doubts about established practices and ideas.
- Provide opportunities for professional development and learning: Organizations can aid their staff in developing the critical thinking skills necessary for success by providing them with many opportunities for professional development.
- Encourage collaboration and diversity of ideas: Employees can gain new insights and creative ideas when they are encouraged to collaborate and exchange thoughts. When people from different backgrounds and cultures work together, it can stimulate more creative problem solving and better decision making.
- Create an environment where it is safe to take risks and fail: Organizations can encourage a culture of critical thinking by providing a setting in which workers are safe to take chances without fear of retaliation. If you fear embarrassment, simply create a safe place to speak privately.
- Recognize and reward critical thinking in decision making and problem-solving: Organizations can encourage people to take a critical thinking approach to decision making and issue solving by recognizing and rewarding employees who display these skills.
- Modeling critical thinking: When it comes to making decisions, resolving issues, and communicating with their teams, managers

and other leaders should demonstrate critical thinking so that others can learn from their example.

Here are a few examples of how organizations can foster a culture of critical thinking:

- Encouraging employees to ask questions and challenge assumptions: In order to encourage employees to think critically, companies should provide them with opportunities to do so. Managers can facilitate open communication by holding meetings at which workers are invited to share their thoughts and ask questions about corporate policy and practice. Also, they can make it so workers feel safe to voice concerns, disapprove views, and offer constructive criticism without fear of retaliation.
- Providing opportunities for professional development and learning: By encouraging employees to take advantage of new learning experiences, companies may create an environment where critical thinking is valued. Workshops, seminars, and training sessions on topics such as analysis, deliberation, problem-solving, and communication could be provided by an organization. As an extra perk, some employers host book clubs or provide employees with lists of suggested reads and other tools to help them develop their critical thinking abilities.
- Encouraging collaboration and diversity of ideas: By promoting teamwork and the exchange of different perspectives, businesses may help employees develop their critical thinking skills. To tackle issues, a company may form cross-functional teams consisting of workers from different departments. In addition, the company may foster an atmosphere where a wide range of viewpoints and experiences are valued and addressed by emphasizing diversity and inclusion.
- Creating an environment where it is safe to take risks and fail: The best way for businesses to encourage employees to think critically is to provide them with a safe space to experiment

without fear of repercussions. When a business creates a safe space for employees to try out new ideas without fear of reprimand, that's an example of a supportive environment. Another way employees might learn to take risks and grow from their missteps is to foster an environment where errors are treated as teaching moments rather than setbacks.

When companies acknowledge and reward employees for using critical thinking in decision making and issue solving, they can help create a culture where such talents are valued and encouraged. An organization may, for instance, have a rewards system in place to encourage and acknowledge individuals who propose novel approaches to old problems. Also, the company may reward workers who show they can use critical thinking to solve problems and make decisions.

Modeling critical thinking

Leaders may encourage a culture of critical thinking in their organizations by using it themselves while making decisions, solving problems, and communicating. Managers and leaders can show they are critical thinkers by including staff in the decision-making process and clarifying their thought processes. In addition, leaders can set the tone by questioning their own ideas and weighing the evidence when approaching a problem. Furthermore, leaders and managers may set a positive example in terms of communication by actively listening to their staff, being open to feedback, and adapting their communication style as necessary. Leaders can foster a culture of critical thinking throughout the organization by following this blueprint themselves.

It's important to keep in mind that fostering an environment where critical thinking is encouraged takes time, energy, and consistency. It's an ongoing procedure that needs input from managers at all levels. It is crucial to monitor the strategy's progress and make adjustments on a regular basis to ensure its continued success. In order to reap the benefits of fostering a culture of critical thinking, businesses should provide chances for employees to hone their critical thinking abilities, promote teamwork, and be recognized for and rewarded for their critical thinking.

An informed workforce that can solve problems creatively and communicate clearly can only be developed by encouraging a culture of critical thinking in the workplace. When companies invest in their employees' ability to think critically, they may better equip them with the tools they need to do their jobs well and contribute to the company's overall success. An organization can foster a culture of critical thinking that benefits decision-making, problem-solving, communication, creativity and innovation, risk management, and more by providing an atmosphere where employees feel safe questioning assumptions, challenging the status quo, and expressing their ideas. Organizations may create a culture of critical thinking and reap the rewards by doing things like praising and acknowledging it, giving chances for professional growth, encouraging cooperation and diversity of ideas, and providing a secure atmosphere for risk-taking and failure.

Questions

1. What are some specific strategies that organizations can use to foster a culture of critical thinking in the workplace?
2. How can an organization create an environment where employees feel comfortable challenging assumptions and expressing dissenting opinions?
3. What are some specific ways in which professional development and learning opportunities can help employees develop critical thinking skills?
4. How can organizations encourage collaboration and diversity of ideas to foster a culture of critical thinking?
5. How can an organization create an environment where employees feel safe taking risks and are not penalized for failure?

PART SEVEN

Critical Thinking in Education

XVII

꧁⚜꧂

Chapter 17: Teaching our Children

"Logic helps us to strip off the outward disguise of things, and to behold and judge of them in their own nature."

—ISAAC WATTS

The ability to think critically is a valuable asset in the classroom, allowing students to more effectively process material, identify and address issues, and arrive at well-considered conclusions. In addition to helping students, teachers can benefit from increasing their own critical thinking abilities by creating and delivering more engaging classes and conducting more reliable assessments of student learning.

Students' ability to think critically can be fostered, in part, by engaging them in open-ended and problem-based learning experiences. Instead of relying solely on rote memorization or rote execution, students engaged in these types of activities are challenged to think critically and creatively to solve challenges. Instead of just giving pupils the information, a science instructor could have them develop an experiment to test a particular scientific hypothesis. Students benefit from this type of learning exercise because it encourages them to think critically and it teaches them about the scientific method and the value of experimentation.

Socratic inquiry is another method for encouraging pupils' growth in analytical thinking. The key is to give kids open-ended questions that require them to elaborate on their answers rather than simply reciting the right one. Instead of merely recalling the events of the past, a history teacher could urge their students to think about what those events might mean now. Students can benefit from Socratic inquiry because it encourages them to think critically about the information they have been given and to consider alternative explanations for the event in question.

Learning to think critically is something that may be developed by teachers themselves via self-reflection and the pursuit of professional growth. One way to improve one's teaching skills is to look for opportunities to do so, as well as to observe other teachers and get feedback from peers. Teachers may, for instance, attend a workshop on the topic to learn more about how to instill critical thinking in their students using methods like Socratic questioning and problem-based learning. Teachers can also benefit from employing critical thinking skills including questioning their own preconceptions and assumptions, opening themselves up to other points of view, and weighing the merits of competing arguments when they design and deliver classes.

Even while it may be difficult to test critical thinking skills, it is not impossible to do so. Instructors can gauge their students' critical thinking abilities in a number of ways. Teachers can evaluate student work more objectively with the use of tools like rubrics, checklists, and score guides that outline clear criteria for what makes strong critical thinking. Moreover, students' ability to think critically can be gauged through formative evaluations like oral and written responses, debates, conversations, and reflections. Tasks that require students to apply, analyze, evaluate, and then generate a product can have a significant impact on the development of students' critical thinking skills provided they are assessed and assisted in the right way.

Educators and students alike can reap many rewards from incorporating critical thinking into the classroom. Children who are able to think critically will be better prepared for a world that is increasingly complex and unpredictable, and teachers will be able to create and deliver more engaging and relevant lessons. In addition, in today's knowledge-based economy, where success is increasingly dependent on a person's capacity for both creative and analytical thought, the development of critical thinking abilities is of paramount importance.

Examples:

1. A high school history teacher assigns students to form groups and create a presentation on a selected historical event by analyzing different perspectives, causes, and consequences of the event.
2. A math teacher gives the students a problem that is not directly related to the curriculum but needs a critical thinking approach to solve it.
3. A middle school social studies teacher assigned students to create a presentation on current events by analyzing different perspectives, causes, and consequences of the events.

To further explore the topic, here are some questions that could be considered with possible solutions:

How can critical thinking skills be integrated into the curriculum across different subject areas?

It is necessary to make a conscious effort to add activities and assignments into the curriculum that develop critical thinking in order to successfully incorporate critical thinking abilities into the curriculum across a variety of topic areas. Here are some ways to integrate critical thinking skills into different subject areas:

- English/Language Arts: Provide your pupils reading and writing assignments that require them to investigate and assess many sources, lines of reasoning, and pieces of evidence. You should try to get them to recognize and examine any assumptions, prejudices, or logical fallacies that they may have.
- Mathematics: Provide students problems with open-ended solutions as well as real-life circumstances that require them to apply their knowledge of mathematics and their ability to think in order to find solutions. Inspire them to explain their rationale and analyze the correctness of their ideas by giving you positive reinforcement.
- Science: In order for pupils to form conclusions, you should encourage them to carry out experiments and investigations, examine data, and evaluate the evidence. Inspire them to consider a variety of potential explanations and theories and to assess those options.
- Social Studies/History: Students should be given research tasks that require them to gather and assess information, consider diverse views, and build arguments that are properly supported. Inspire others to challenge their preconceived notions, prejudices, and stereotypes.
- Arts: Inspire your kids to think critically about pieces of art, music, and literature that they encounter. Inspire them to assess the persuasiveness of the artist's message, as well as to recognize and examine any preconceptions, biases, or stereotypes that they may hold.

In general, incorporating critical thinking skills into the curriculum calls for a concerted effort from educators in a variety of subject areas to work together in order to construct learning environments that support and encourage the development of critical thinking abilities.

What are the barriers to implementing critical thinking in education and how can they be overcome?

- Lack of training: Some educators may not know how to impart the value of critical thinking to their students. They might not know how to think critically either.
- Emphasis on standardized testing: The emphasis on standardized testing in many school systems may leave little time for developing students' capacity for critical thinking.
- Lack of resources: There is a risk that educators lack the tools they need to instill critical thinking in their students.
- Resistance to change: Some teachers may be reluctant to modify their practices in order to include critical thinking into the classroom since they have been using the same strategies for many years and have found them to be efficient.

To overcome these barriers, it is important to:

- Provide training: Teachers should receive training on how to teach critical thinking skills and how to integrate critical thinking into their teachings.
- Redefine success: The concept of success in educational systems should be rethought to incorporate not only performance on standardized tests but also the capacity for critical thinking.
- Provide resources: Textbooks and other forms of educational technology should be made available to instructors in order to facilitate the teaching of critical thinking in schools.
- Encourage collaboration: It is important for educators to work together to exchange concepts and approaches for instructing

students in critical thinking, as well as to provide one another with support as they make adjustments to the ways in which they educate.

- Start early: Students should begin learning the skills necessary for critical thinking at an early age so that they can gradually develop these talents through time and be better equipped to apply them in higher education and in their future employment. When instructing an older pupil, it is important to begin as soon as feasible and to accommodate them as often as possible.

How can teachers effectively assess critical thinking skills in students?

It might be difficult to evaluate pupils' critical thinking abilities, but there are a few strategies that have proven to be helpful, including the following:

- Rubrics: The criteria for critical thinking can be clearly defined with the help of teachers who can design rubrics that also provide grading scales for each of the criteria.
- Assignments: Students can be given tasks that challenge them to display critical thinking skills, such as assessing an argument or finding a solution to a difficult problem. These tasks can be designed by teachers.
- Classroom discussion: Instructors are able to assess student participation in class debates, including the strength of their arguments and their capacity to think critically about the points of view of others.
- Performance-based assessments: The use of performance-based assessments in the classroom, like debates or simulations, which force students to apply their critical thinking abilities in an authentic setting, is something that teachers can do.
- Portfolios: Students can be asked to produce a portfolio of their

work that displays their progress in critical thinking over the course of the school year by their teachers.

It is essential for instructors to clearly convey the expectations they have for students' critical thinking skills and to provide continuous feedback to their pupils. Teachers are able to obtain a more in-depth comprehension of their students' capacities for critical thinking when they make use of a wide range of evaluation strategies.

In what ways can critical thinking skills be beneficial for students in the long run, both in academic and non-academic settings?

Students can gain a lot of value from developing their critical thinking skills in a variety of different contexts, both academic and non-academic ones. The following is a list of the ways in which students can benefit in the long run from developing skills in critical thinking:

- Improved academic performance: Students who are able to better grasp and evaluate the academic information they are studying will have an easier time performing well in their classes and on their tests if they have developed their critical thinking skills.
- Better problem-solving skills: Students who are able to acquire strong critical thinking abilities are better suited to address complicated problems in a number of situations, whether they are in the academic world or the professional world.
- Improved decision-making: Students can improve their ability to make informed judgments by studying and evaluating the information that is accessible by developing their critical thinking skills.
- Increased creativity: Pupils who cultivate their abilities in critical thinking are better equipped to think creatively and find original answers to challenging questions.
- Improved communication skills: Students who have developed

their critical thinking skills may find that they are better able to express their ideas and thoughts in both written and verbal form.
- Better career prospects: Skills in critical thinking are highly valued by employers, and students who possess these skills are more likely to be successful in the jobs that they choose later in life.

Students, in general, can stand to gain from improving their critical thinking skills in a variety of contexts, including academic and non-academic ones, which will ultimately put them up for success in the long run.

How does the development of critical thinking skills in teachers influence the classroom environment and the student learning experience?

The cultivation of critical thinking abilities in educators has the potential to have a substantial impact on the atmosphere of the classroom as well as the educational experience of the students. Teachers who themselves have well-developed capacities for critical thinking are in a better position to encourage the development of those capacities in their pupils. They are able to devise learning activities for students that require them to engage in the processes of information analysis, assessment, and synthesis, as well as the use of evidence to support their beliefs.

When teachers have strong critical thinking skills, they are more likely to create an environment in which students feel encouraged to ask questions, challenge assumptions, and take intellectual risks. This is because teachers who have strong critical thinking skills are more likely to create an environment in that their pupils exhibit strong critical thinking skills. This kind of atmosphere in the classroom can result in higher levels of student involvement and motivation, in addition to improved academic achievements. In addition, educators who serve as models of critical thinking can assist students in the development of essential life skills such as effective communication, problem-solving, and decision-making, all of which are highly valued in academic as well as non-academic contexts. In general, the cultivation of analytical thinking abilities among educators is absolutely necessary for the formation of a constructive and productive educational setting that is conducive to the achievement of students.

It is essential to keep in mind that the cultivation of critical thinking abilities is not a one-time occurrence but rather an ongoing process that takes place over time. The commitment to consistently fostering and modeling critical thinking abilities is a responsibility that falls on educators, students, and educational institutions alike. It is also very important to give students plenty of opportunity and resources to hone their ability to think critically and apply what they have learned. In addition, there should be consistent review and evaluation of the efficacy of the implementation of critical thinking skills in order to identify areas in which there is room for development.

The educational system presents a number of opportunities to foster and practice critical thinking, which is a highly useful talent. Teachers can assist students in developing their critical thinking abilities by giving them opportunities for open-ended and problem-based learning, employing Socratic questioning, and promoting metacognition. Teachers can also improve their own critical thinking abilities by actively seeking out opportunities for professional development, engaging in practice-based reflection, and incorporating critical thinking strategies while planning and delivering instruction for their students. In addition, conducting regular assessments of students' critical thinking abilities enables teachers to gain useful insights into their students' learning and to tailor their lessons accordingly.

Questions

1. How can critical thinking skills be integrated into the curriculum?
2. What are the barriers to implementing critical thinking in education?
3. How can teachers assess critical thinking skills in students?
4. In what ways can critical thinking skills be beneficial for students in the long run?
5. How does the development of critical thinking skills in teachers influence the classroom environment?

XVIII

Chapter 18: Teaching the Teachers

"The function of education is to teach one to think intensively and to think critically. Intelligence plus character."

—MARTIN LUTHER KING JR.

For Teachers and HomeSchool Parents:

As educators, it is essential for us to model and foster critical thinking skills in our students. Teaching is not only about imparting knowledge, but also about equipping students with the skills to navigate the complexities of the world around them. Critical thinking skills are essential for success in the 21st century, and as teachers, we play a vital role in developing these skills in our students.

To start, teachers can benefit greatly from engaging in regular reflective practice. Reflective practice allows us to analyze and evaluate our own teaching methods and identify areas for improvement. It is a powerful tool that can be used to evaluate the effectiveness of teaching strategies, such as the use of open-ended questions, problem-based learning, or Socratic questioning. Through reflection, teachers can identify areas of strength and areas that need more attention, and use this information to inform their instruction and help students to develop critical thinking skills.

Another way teachers can develop their own critical thinking skills is by participating in professional development opportunities. Workshops, seminars, and other professional development opportunities provide teachers with new strategies and ideas on how to integrate critical thinking into their instruction. For example, a teacher might attend a workshop on teaching critical thinking skills, where they learn about different strategies for teaching critical thinking, such as the use of Socratic questioning, or the use of problem-based learning.

In the classroom, teachers can promote critical thinking skills by using a variety of strategies that foster active, student-centered learning. Socratic questioning is one such strategy, where teachers ask open-ended questions that encourage students to think deeper about a topic, rather than simply providing a correct answer. Discussions are another powerful tool, where students are encouraged to share their ideas and perspectives and engage in respectful dialogue. By creating an environment where students feel comfortable expressing their opinions and challenging one another's ideas, teachers can help students to develop their critical thinking skills.

Cooperative learning is also a valuable strategy that can be used to promote critical thinking skills. Cooperative learning is an instructional method where students work in small groups to solve problems or complete projects. By working together, students are encouraged to share ideas and learn from one another, which helps to develop critical thinking skills.

Additionally, problem-based learning is also an effective approach that provides students with real-world problems or challenges to solve, which promotes critical thinking by encouraging students to analyze and evaluate information, solve problems, and make informed decisions.

When it comes to assessment, critical thinking skills can be challenging to measure, but it is not impossible. Teachers can use a variety of assessment strategies to evaluate student's critical thinking skills, such as rubrics, checklists, and scoring guides that provide clear criteria for what constitutes good critical thinking. Formative assessments such as oral and written responses, debates, discussions, and reflections can provide a good indication of student's critical thinking skills.

Developing critical thinking skills as a teacher is a crucial step towards fostering a critical thinking culture in the classroom and equipping students with the skills they need to be successful in the 21st century. Reflective practice, professional development opportunities, the use of open-ended questions and discussions, PBL, and the use of Socratic questioning, are all powerful strategies that can help teachers to develop their own critical thinking skills and create an environment that encourages critical thinking among students.

For Trainers and Managers:

As trainers or managers in education, it is essential to understand the importance of critical thinking and to develop strategies for promoting critical thinking skills among educators and students.

One way to promote critical thinking skills among educators is by providing ongoing professional development opportunities that focus on the teaching of critical thinking. This can include workshops, seminars, or online training sessions where educators can learn about different strategies for teaching critical thinking, such as the use of Socratic questioning or problem-based learning. By providing ongoing professional development opportunities, managers and trainers can ensure that educators have the skills and knowledge they need to integrate critical thinking into their instruction and create a culture of critical thinking in their classrooms.

Another way to promote critical thinking skills is by providing educators with the tools and resources they need to foster a critical thinking culture in their classrooms. This might include providing access to critical thinking instructional materials or curricula, or offering coaching and mentoring to help educators integrate critical thinking into their instruction. Managers and trainers can also provide educators with opportunities to observe and learn from other educators who have experience teaching critical thinking.

One way to do this is by providing students with opportunities to engage in problem-based learning, where they are presented with real-world problems to solve and are encouraged to analyze and evaluate information, solve problems, and make informed decisions. Another way is to provide students with opportunities for open-ended and discovery-based learning, where students are encouraged to think critically and creatively and come up with their own solutions to problems.

Assessment of critical thinking skills can be challenging, but it is not impossible. Managers and trainers can work with educators to develop assessment tools that measure critical thinking skills, such as rubrics, checklists, and scoring guides that provide clear criteria for what constitutes good critical thinking. They can also encourage the use of formative assessments such as oral and written responses, debates, discussions, and reflections which can provide a good indication of student's critical thinking skills.

In addition, managers and trainers can also promote critical thinking skills within their own organizations. This might include encouraging critical thinking and problem-solving as part of the decision-making process, or promoting a culture of continuous improvement that encourages employees to think critically about their work and identify areas for improvement. Additionally, managers and trainers can also promote critical thinking by providing opportunities for employees to work on complex, multi-disciplinary projects that require them to think creatively and analytically.

Another important aspect of promoting critical thinking in education is to ensure that the curriculum and instruction are aligned with critical thinking goals. Managers and trainers should ensure that the curriculum and instruction focus on the development of critical thinking skills, and that the curriculum includes open-ended and problem-based learning activities that require students to think critically and creatively. They should also ensure that educators are provided with the resources they need to teach critical thinking skills and that assessment of critical thinking skills is integrated into the curriculum.

Managers and trainers can also promote critical thinking by encouraging ongoing research and evaluation. This might include conducting studies to examine the effectiveness of different instructional strategies, or evaluating the impact of critical thinking instruction on student learning outcomes. By conducting research and evaluation, managers and trainers can identify best practices for promoting critical thinking and make data-driven decisions about how to improve instruction.

Examples:

1. A manager of an organization provides ongoing professional development opportunities for staff focusing on teaching critical thinking skills.
2. A training manager encourages ongoing research and evaluation within the organization to identify best practices for promoting critical thinking among educators.

As trainers or managers, it is essential to understand the importance of critical thinking and to develop strategies for promoting critical thinking skills among educators, students, and within their own organizations. This can be achieved through ongoing professional development opportunities, providing educators with the tools and resources they need to foster a critical thinking culture in their classrooms, providing students with opportunities to engage in problem-based and open-ended learning, encouraging critical thinking within the decision-making process and promoting a culture of continuous improvement and encouraging ongoing research and evaluation.

Questions

For Teachers:

1. How can teachers use reflective practice as a tool to improve their lessons and help students learn how to think critically?
2. What are some examples of professional development opportunities that teachers can take part in to learn how to teach critical thinking?
3. How can Socratic questioning be used in the classroom to encourage students to think critically? What are some examples of open-ended questions that can be used to get students to think more deeply?
4. How does cooperative learning help students learn to think critically, and what are some cooperative learning activities that can be used in the classroom?
5. How can you test a student's ability to think critically? How can formative assessments, like oral and written responses, debates, discussions, and reflections, show how well a student can think critically?

For Trainers and Managers:

1. What are some ways to help trainers and your students learn how to think critically?
2. How can opportunities for ongoing professional development help trainers and managers add critical thinking to what they teach?
3. What tools and resources can managers and trainers give to help build a culture of critical thinking in your facility?
4. How can managers and trainers tell if a student is able to think critically?
5. How can managers and trainers in their own organizations encourage people to think critically?

PART EIGHT

Critical Thinking and Public Speaking

XIX

Chapter 19: Debates and Public Speaking

"A wise man speaks because he has something to say, a fool speaks because he has to say something."

—PLATO

Whether you need to give a presentation at business, give a speech at a conference, or just take part in a class discussion, the ability to speak in front of a group is a vital talent in today's society. One must not only be well-versed in verbal and nonverbal communication but also take a critical stance toward public speaking if they hope to succeed at it. By doing so, presenters may guarantee that their arguments are well-organized and convincing, and that they get their point over to the listeners.

The ability to recognize and assess arguments is a crucial part of critical thinking for public speakers. An argument is a piece of evidence that is used to back up a claim or a conclusion. Knowing the distinction between a solid argument and a weak one is essential for any public speaker. Arguments that are well-reasoned and backed up by facts are considered good, whereas those that rely on the speaker's opinions and feelings are deemed to be fallacious.

While delivering a speech, it's crucial that you articulate your central claim and back it up with evidence. This will aid the listeners in grasping the speech's central argument and supporting details. The evidence presented should be credible and pertinent to the discussion at hand, both of which the speaker should assess. This involves determining if the evidence is relevant to the argument, if there are any biases in the sources, and if the sources themselves are credible. This will show the listeners that you've thought critically about the debate and researched your points thoroughly.

The ability to recognize and reject logical fallacies is another facet of critical thinking in public speaking. Any argument can be weakened by the use of fallacies, which are logical errors in reasoning. Ad hominem is when you attack the person instead of the argument; appeal to authority is when you use the opinion of an authority figure to bolster your argument without evidence; and strawman is when you distort an opposing perspective to make it easier to rebut.

Examples of fallacies in public speaking:

1. During a political discussion, one candidate will accuse their rival of being dishonest, but they will not provide any evidence to back up their claim. This is an illustration of the fallacy known as "ad hominem."
2. The benefits of a new medication are touted in a presentation, and a prominent physician is cited as a source. However, the speaker gives no information on the physician's credentials or experience with the medication being discussed. That reasoning is a classic case of the error of appealing to authority.
3. A student participates in a discussion with their classmates about

a new school regulation. Throughout the course of the conversation, the student asserts that the policy should not be implemented since it will be very restrictive. This is an illustration of the logical fallacy known as the straw man.

As a public speaker, it is essential to be familiar with these logical fallacies and to steer clear of employing them in your own arguments whenever possible. To achieve this goal, it is essential to make use of tools for critical thinking, such as Toulmin's model of argumentation. This model can assist the speakers in organizing the argument and locating and analyzing the claims, evidence, and assumptions that are being made in the argument. By doing so, speakers can steer clear of logical fallacies and provide the audience with a more convincing argument. Additionally, using preemptive counter arguments, which means anticipating and addressing potential objections to your argument in advance, can assist speakers in avoiding fallacies and building credibility with the audience. This is because preemptive counter arguments require speakers to anticipate and address potential objections to their argument.

Toulmin's Model of Argumentation

To elaborate, Toulmin's model of argumentation is a method for breaking down arguments and re-creating them in new contexts. Claim, data or evidence, warrant, backing, rebuttal, and qualifier are the six primary components that make up this structure.

- Claim: The main point or conclusion that the argument is trying to make.
- Data/evidence: The evidence, whether it be statistics, examples, or facts, that are presented in support of the claim.
- Warrant: The rationale or assumption that underlies the claim and establishes its validity.

- Backing: Anything that may be added to the warrant's argument to bolster it would be very helpful.
- Rebuttal: Counter Arguments or objections that could be raised in response to the argument.
- Qualifier: An acknowledgement of the limitations or conditions within which the argument may be valid.

By doing an analysis of an argument utilizing these components, we are able to gain a better understanding of the argument's strengths and shortcomings as well as places in which the argument could be strengthened by the addition of more evidence or reasoning. If we develop an argument employing these components, we will be able to create an argument that is more convincing and more successful.

Examples of using critical thinking tools in public speaking:

1. A business presenter will utilize Toulmin's model to frame their argument and provide a logical and convincing case for a new venture while they are making a presentation to their audience.
2. A candidate prepares for and responds to any objections to their viewpoint during a political debate. This demonstrates to the audience that the candidate has given careful consideration to a variety of points of view and has a comprehensive comprehension of the matter at hand.

Here are two scenarios that expand on these ideas:

Example One: When delivering a presentation on a new product, a business expert uses Toulmin's model to outline the argument that they are presenting.

During the course of the presentation, the business expert will start by describing the issue at hand and the reasons why a new product is required. After that, he makes the claim, which is that the latest product is the answer to the issue that has been bothering them. After that, he proceeds to substantiate his assertion with supporting evidence. This evidence consists of facts on the product's performance as well as testimonials from previous customers. In addition to this, he offers a warrant, which can be thought of as a guiding principle or an assumption that relates the claim to the evidence. In this instance, the guarantee is that the product is dependable, effective, and efficient from a financial standpoint. In the end, he arrives at a conclusion, which is that the latest product is the most effective approach to resolving the issue. When a business expert makes use of Toulmin's model, they are able to offer an argument that is crystal clear and logical, and their audience is able to comprehend and follow the reasoning that lies behind the assertion.

Example Two: When discussing a contentious political issue in front of his peers, a college student steers clear of the ad hominem fallacy by avoiding personal attacks on those who hold the opposing perspective.

Throughout their speech, the college student recognizes the opposing opinion, but rather of criticizing the person or group who holds that viewpoint, they focus on the evidence and logical reasoning to support their own argument rather than attacking the person or group who holds that viewpoint. The student demonstrates that they have adopted a critical stance by not only providing counterarguments but also refuting those arguments using valid logical reasoning. In addition, the student stays on subject and avoids making any personal attacks, which helps to maintain the audience's attention on the matter at hand and the arguments that are being presented rather than on the individual who is giving them. The student will be able to maintain their credibility and integrity as well as deliver an argument that is well-reasoned, logical, and convincing to the audience if they refrain from using the ad hominem fallacy.

The ability to think critically is one of the most important aspects of effective public speaking. By applying the principles of critical thinking to the process of public speaking, speakers can ensure that their arguments are understandable, logical, and convincing, and that they are able to effectively communicate their message to the audience. [Critical thinking] [is] a subset of [the] broader [field of] critical thinking. Speakers can improve their public speaking skills, increase their credibility, and enhance the effectiveness of their message by improving their ability to identify and evaluate arguments, avoiding common fallacies, or utilizing critical thinking tools such as Toulmin's model of argumentation and pre-emptive counter arguments. All of these things can be done to improve critical thinking skills.

The application of critical thinking in public speaking is not confined to the actual delivery of the speech; rather, it is an ongoing process that begins with the production of ideas and continues through preparation, research, and the delivery of the speech itself. To be able to approach public speaking in a critical manner, it is therefore vital for speakers to develop their capacity for critical thinking and to become familiar with the fundamental principles and tools that are involved. Using the principles of critical thinking and taking an analytical approach are effective ways to improve one's ability to express ideas, persuade others, and advocate for a cause during public speaking. Public speaking is not simply about communicating facts.

The most important thing that one should take away from reading this chapter is the realization that having the capacity to think logically is an essential and transferable talent that can be used to all aspects of life, including giving speeches in public. You will improve as a public speaker in terms of self-assurance, efficiency, and persuasion if you work on increasing your critical thinking skills. Furthermore, do not forget what I mentioned in a previous chapter, you must have clear definitions so that your argument can be sound to the audience.

Questions

1. How can you apply the Toulmin model of argumentation in your next public speaking opportunity?
2. Can you think of a time when you've seen a fallacy used in a public speaking context (remember to check your personal bias)? How could the speaker have approached it differently using critical thinking?
3. How can you anticipate and address potential counter arguments in your next public speaking opportunity?
4. In what ways can you incorporate critical thinking into your speech to make it more persuasive?
5. How can you practice identifying and evaluating arguments and avoiding fallacies in your daily life, outside of public speaking?

PART NINE

Case Studies

XX

❦

Chapter 20: Case Studies Introduction

"...I learned to read carefully and not be satisfied with a rough understanding of the whole, and not to agree too quickly with those who have a lot to say about something."

—MARCUS AURELIUS, MEDITATIONS, 1.7.3

People need to realize that writing is a fundamental talent for everyone who wants to develop a logical, critical thinking mind. Writing down your views and analyzing the scenario can help you see your biases more clearly and create better structures. If you don't include this, you'll be more susceptible to the impact of misinformed social media, friends, and family. These writings, which I've dubbed "case studies," were written both for myself and for whoever happens to read them. In doing so, I hope to demonstrate my perspective on a variety of timely issues and equip you with tools for conducting your own research and analysis.

Writing down your ideas and organizing them using the techniques you learned previously does not require you to be a professional writer or even to have a firm grasp of basic grammatical fundamentals. Think of it like a journal for your logical mind. Put it to work clarifying and simplifying things for you. I hope by now you understand why I have asked you questions throughout the book and work are way to this portion. It is to get used to the idea of this critical step, writing.

Case Study I: Cultural Immersion and Supremacy

"Give us the child for 8 years and it will be a Bolshevik forever"

—VLADIMIR LENIN

[During the lockdowns that occurred in 2020, this essay was the first of many that were written. A variety of corporate news channels were reporting on a series of occurrences that were giving me cause for concern. In my capacity as a critical thinker, I considered that the most reasonable course of action would be to examine, look for evidence, and provide support for my hypothesis regarding these themes. The first is that the concept of "white supremacy" was attached to the idea of being a hard worker. As a person of Hispanic heritage who takes pride in working away at worthwhile endeavors, I felt this to be pretty condescending. The greatest strategy, which I emphasized throughout the whole book, is to approach subjects with a logical mindset and to think critically about them. In addition to this, it is necessary for you to write down your thoughts rather than keeping them in your head, where they can become muddled and irrational.]

I had a particular interest in special operations while training to be an Army officer. Counter-Terrorism/Intelligence was one in particular. Culture immersions are part of the training for some of these units. That is, trainees are sent to live, eat, speak, and absorb the culture. This was discovered to be the most effective strategy to achieve success in that country. Yet, as a society, we have been trained differently in the United States. We are encouraged to adapt to other cultures in the United States. Now, whether or not it is the appropriate road to take is debatable, but what I find hazardous is supporting racism as the primary source of a society. The "White Dominant Culture (Anti-Whiteness)" chart on exhibit at The National Museum of African American History and Culture is one example of this (a wing of the prestigious Smithsonian). This paper was short-lived and removed at the time of writing, although it is still being discussed[17]. This chart showed SOME of the following (in case it is lost in time):

- Rugged Individualism:
    - The Individual is the primary unit
    - Self-Reliance
    - Independence & autonomy highly valued and rewarded
- Family Structure:
    - The nuclear family: father, mother, 2.3 children is the ideal social unit
    - Children should have own rooms, be independent
- Emphasis on Scientific Method:
    - Objective, rational linear thinking
    - Cause and effect relationships
- History:
    - Base on immigrants' experience in the United States
    - The primacy of (Western Greek, Roman) and Judeo-Christian Tradition
- Protestant Work Ethic:
    - Hard work is the key to success
    - "If you didn't meet your goals, you didn't work hard enough"
- Religion:
    - Christianity is the norm
    - No tolerance for deviation from single God concept
- Status, Power, and Authority:
    - Respect Authority
    - Heavy value on ownership of goods, space, property
- Future Orientation:
    - Plan for the Future
    - Delayed Gratification
- Time:
    - Follow rigid time schedule
    - Time viewed as a commodity
- Aesthetics:
    - Women's beauty based on blonde, thin -"Barbie"
    - Man's attractiveness based on economic status, power, intellect
- Holidays:
    - Based on Christian religions
    - Based on white history & male leaders
- Justice:
    - Based on English common law
    - Protect property and entitlements
- Competition:
    - Be #1

- ○ Decision-Making
- Communication:
  - ○ "The King's English" rules
  - ○ Be Polite

There is substantially more to this list in which you may see for yourself in the references section but this list describes "whiteness". They later removed this exhibit and apologized for the offensive post. The fact that the Smithsonian authorized such a ludicrous notion that this list, which is proven throughout history from a VARI-ETY of cultures around the world, is called "whiteness" profoundly disturbed me.

To elaborate, I look to Feudal Japan, the one culture, race, and civilization that shared identical principles yet was (historically speaking) the furthest removed from any European nation in the globe. Japan is perhaps one of the most idealized feudal countries. In comparison, their honor, codes, and passion for perfection were unparalleled. Many claim that this is why, as of this writing, teens in Japan continue to have one of the highest suicide rates among affluent countries[18]. Shintoism and Bushido are two of their culture's founding reasons. Now, I will not make many comparisons from Judeo-Christianity, except to note that, with the exception of God vs Gods, the similarities to being "blessed" and redemption (asking for forgiveness) do exist. Bushido, on the other hand, has a distinct comparison to "whiteness," as the museum so etiquette described it. When it came to studies, religion was where most educational systems taught moral lessons. Beginning in the 1980s, we in America began to shift to a new sort of moral lessons through social justice. Yet, religion was not necessarily taught in schools in Japan from the 17th through the early 20th centuries, but Bushido was (shinto religion was performed rather than simply taught). Bushido is a moral as well as a virtue code. Bushido translates to "warrior's way" in Japanese. Samurai life was harsh for any human being. According to Inazo Nitobe, author of "Code of the Samurai," "Children of tender age were sent among utter strangers with some message to deliver, were made to rise before the sun, and before breakfast attend to their reading exercises, walking to their teacher with bare feet in the cold of winter; they frequently-once or twice a month, as on the festival of a god of learning- came together in small groups and pass the night without sleep, in remembrance of the god of I can't make up an example of hard effort and respect for authority if this isn't it.

Notwithstanding this way of life, another aspect of Bushido is Benevolence. Benevolence is characterized as "love, magnanimity, affection for others, sympathy and pity, were ever regarded to be supreme virtues..." in another Bushido virtue. Being polite is important in Japanese culture, and it is the fourth virtue of Bushido. Furthermore, the Bushido acknowledges the distinction between being courteous out of fear of offending someone and being genuinely polite (the ultimate kind), which approaches love. This may be related to the extreme political correctness prevalent in North America today. Bushido also goes into great detail about Honor, Loyalty, Justice, and Self-Control[19] [20]. The fact that the Japanese, who banned all foreign visitors from 1603 to 1867 (except the Dutch, who were allowed once a year for trade)[21] managed to have traits similar to "whiteness" may indicate that the inductive reasoning behind the "white dominant culture" chart (broad generalizations from specific observations) was not only inaccurate but also dangerous logical fallacies. But then I saw it was more than just twisting truths for reeducation; it appeared to me to be an intellectual revolution through brainwashing. This list is nearly identical to the Communist Manifesto and Lenin's philosophy[22] [23] [24].

The Smithsonian display, by coincidence, mimics another type of thought. Individualism is strongly opposed in the Marxism/Lenin Doctrine because it goes against the community or social group. You are also just as successful as your community or social group permits you to be. In other words, if you aspire to be number one or the best, you will either get in trouble for leaving the group or the group will be reprimanded for not performing as well as that individual. It is true that the bottom percentage of the population rises slightly, but almost every historical "simulation" has come at the expense of ingenuity, individual identity (unless you are the leader, in which case you take the credit), and instability because almost all resources are finite to some extent. Yet, remember, in most communist revolutions, those who climb to a position of some influence and may challenge the communist revolutionary's leader are usually slain. Let us not forget the tremendous genocide that claimed the lives of well over 100 million people simply because they were different or expressed uniqueness[25]. Marx stated that individualism is the ideology of the ruling class[26], which justifies every communist's use of force to force change and conformity.

So, is this "White Dominant Culture" chart a true representation of white superiority over the nation, or is it communist propaganda telling all people of color that "if you think like an individual, you are the dominant culture"? After analyzing this and other civilizations, such as Japanese culture, it is safe to say that this chart's inductive reasoning was utterly incorrect. Additionally, the fact that an institution such as The Smithsonian gave this list legitimacy, even for a short time, will reverberate in the thoughts of people who applauded and were affected by it. This document resembles Communist philosophy that I have never seen at an educational institution. If we just included the words "color people can't/can't have: _____," it would be branded the most racist document to people of color produced in my lifetime. It is more difficult to admit that hard work, punctuality, and politeness are necessary for success in this world. Try doing business in Asian countries without it if you don't believe me. My personal wish for you is to learn different cultures, appreciate your own, and be yourself. Strive to be a master of your trade and accept responsibility for your life, much like the Samurai.

Questions

1. **Reflect on Culture:** Many Critical Theorists believe culture can not be exchanged through experience. Marco Polo, the italian explorer who lived in asia for years, embraced the asian culture (one of the very few instances an outsider was accepted before the 20th century) and brought noodles which became pasta; Muslum jihad, prior to the catholic crusades, inspired a European revolution of Science and Mathematics; U.S. Government clandestine training involves cultural immersion which is having agents live in the environments that they are going to be working in; South Koreans have defeated Americans in international hip hop dancing several times despite the fact it was the Black American communities who invented and evolved the style. Regardless of these radical examples, many believe culture should still be divided. Describe, in your own words, how culture immersion can hinder AND benefit your own culture?
   1. Debate on these topics or write an argument to support your findings.
      1. **TIP:** Fold a piece of paper in half and write: Pro and Con. Find facts that support your Pro/Con.
2. **Question:** Why would a Marxist prefer segregation within a collective group over individualism and cultural immersion? Explain, in your own words, why people would believe in the idea of individualism as an oppressive idea? Find examples to support your claim.
   1. **NOTE:** Research psychological behaviors of abusers, cultists, social groups, and societies that have been successful throughout history (how people were treated is the key).
3. **Small Project-Based Practice:** Investigate 3 non-Caucasian historical figures who displayed the traits listed within the "White Dominant Culture" chart. Describe how these traits benefited these historical figures. Remember to back up your findings with examples and facts.
   1. **TIP:** You can start with a search of a country that interests you. Then look for their leaders or heroes who made an impact on that country.

Case Study II: Changing History For The Sake of "Truth" over facts

"History will be kind to me for I intend to write it."

—WINSTON CHURCHILL

[As a history teacher, I was proud of three things: my understanding of history, my ability to teach students critical thinking skills, and my encouragement of students to seek information outside of the assigned textbooks, which nearly always contain some bias within the text. When the 1619 Project gained popularity and I became aware of the erroneous arguments, I immediately tried to prevent others from taking it seriously. Furthermore, there were only a few references to back up the author's assertion, and many notable historians have already dismissed the work due to its use of fallacies, lack of context, and misunderstanding of history. However, beginning in 2023, a show will be accessible to reinforce the paper's principles and teach future generations that history rather than actual history.]

To begin, Native Americans, not Africans, were the first slaves in America. Native People, for the most part, were not only tough to enslave, but they also knew the land and other tribes. This is a well-documented fact in American history. More specifically, the first natives to be enslaved were Taínos, my ancestors (around 1493-1508 depending on whether you date Christopher Columbus or Ponce de Leon)[27]. Although moving away from the practice of enslaving Indigenous people, Spain began importing African slaves and employing indentured workers as a new way of life[28]. Many Europeans exchanged their life for various reasons, such as debt or the potential of a fresh opportunity. Yet, because the life expectancy and standard of living were so low, they perished before their indentured servitude was fulfilled.

The Columbian Exchange, which subsequently became the Atlantic (Triangular) Exchange, followed[29]. This is the beginning of the "1619 project's" history[30].

Slavery's complexities can be traced back to the beginning of recorded history (Sumer in Mesopotamia)[31]. Yet, some of the best western evidence of slavery can be found in Rome and Egypt, with the Israelites (Jews) enslaved by the Egyptians. The pyramids were built by slaves. The power vacuum in African nations occurred after the demise of the great Roman empire (an empire that possessed slaves). Slavery was not only tolerated, but for the majority of people, it was the way the world worked. One-third of the population in African nations (historically known as Senegambia) was enslaved[32]. Furthermore, during their Jihad (before the Crusades of the Vatican), Muslim nations enslaved numerous white or olive-skinned Christians[33]. Slaves were exchanged for weaponry in order to continue the fight on their rival African states. I'll go into more detail later, but these facts alone call the "1619 Project" Veracity into doubt. Yet, receiving a Pulitzer Prize lends legitimacy to an essay that contained no factual proof and was merely an interpretation of history through a very narrow lens.

Here are some statistics: African slaves were enslaved first by other Africans, and if not sold for international trade, they were employed for chattel/agriculture, military duty, or local trading. As a matter of fact, the first African slave purchased in Jamestown was by Anthony Johnson, a free black man and former indentured servant who was a large plantation owner. Nevertheless, These slaves were capable men, women, and children who, in many cases, were in the wrong place at the wrong time and were silenced and enslaved by a larger force. They were also no fools. Boston was the site of the first immunization in the American colonies. A slave named "Onesimus" (own-esimus) in Boston, who was owned by a Puritan clergyman named Cotton Mather, provided Smallpox vaccine and later taught others how to do so. Later, he was credited with preserving the Boston colony[34]. Phillis Wheatley was another strong-willed slave. She was bought in Boston to be a house servant, but according to stories and journals, she was more of an adopted daughter who was not only emancipated but also schooled in English, Roman, and Greek. She was the first African American and one of the first women to publish a book of poetry in her period. "A ardent supporter of America's war for independence, Wheatley produced several poems in praise of the Continental Army's commander, George Washington," according to her biography. Wheatley submitted one of these works, penned in 1775, to the future president, prompting him to invite him to his headquarters in Cambridge, Massachusetts. Wheatley accepted the invitation and traveled to Washington in March 1776."[35] [36]. Slaves also introduced practices that produced modern medicine, meals, and musical culture that we witness today, such as music that inspired nearly every modern popular sound in the United States to spanish music, such as Salsa and Merengue[37].

Furthermore, slaves introduced a new definition of bravery into the new world. Consider the case of James Armistead. Born into slavery, he rose to not only stand by George Washington and Marquis de La Fayette, but was also the first double spy in America, and is credited with being the pivotal individual in the Colonial Army's success. He obtained a full pension and was granted his freedom[38]. There are many other outstanding leaders who sprang up from slavery but I will address that further in another section "History, the lifeblood society".

Some argue that slaves who remained in Africa were treated better, and that if they realized the cruel environment they would be entering, they would refuse to sell to merchants. If that were the case, modern-day slavery, such as child labor, sex trade, and forced labor, would not exist today[39].

Slavery has existed from the 18th century BC in Babylon and 10,000 BC in Mesopotamia. It has since spread across cultures, religions, and nationalities. Furthermore, the social, economic, and legal status of slaves varied depending on the culture and age in which it occurred. We must not forget that the Egyptian pyramids were erected by Israeli slaves. Furthermore, many people, particularly during the Roman Empire, bonded themselves into slavery to pay off debts. Some slave gladiators were willing slaves who volunteered for the chance at glory. With the exception of a few cultures, it became less widespread throughout the early Middle Ages after the fall of Rome. Examining this further, Christians were enslaved during the Byzantine-Ottoman wars of 1265-1479 and the Ottoman conflicts in Europe between the 14th and 20th centuries. From the seventh through the twentieth centuries, many African-Arab kingdoms ruled over areas ranging from Western and Central Asia to Northern and Eastern Africa, Europe, and India. This was close to the time of the Atlantic slave trade. This resulted in a new form of enslavement. Originally, this new form was not about race, but rather about "chattel" servitude. This classifies humans as goods rather than human beings. Individuals in bonds, as well as their progeny, will remain in bonds. When the Portuguese and West African nations began trafficking slaves in the mid-1400s, this was invented. Because of the slave trade, kingdoms such as Dahomey and Ashanti rose to prominence. They were so successful that they started collecting individuals further inland. However, in the United States, many Christians began to justify slavery on the basis of race and moral ideals rather than just property, which exacerbated the situation. When something becomes a moral value, it becomes the "proper thing to do" and can thus become hostile when that moral value is defiled.

Notwithstanding these facts, the 1619 Project undermines a fundamental issue confronting the world today: modern-day slavery. Millions of children and adults are enslaved in every country on the planet! These modern-day slaves are exploited both personally and commercially. What is more alarming is that it is easily accessible. These can include those who make our clothes, labor in factories, clean our homes, pick our crops, or provide services such as food and cosmetics. I'm not even talking about people being underpaid! I'm talking about the truest type of slavery that involves bondage and dread. From the outside, these employees appear to be performing routine tasks. Yet, the people are controlled by violence, the confiscation of passports, the inability to escape debt, and/or the fear of deportation. Here are a list of modern day slaves taken shape:

- Forced labor: work and/or services people are forced to do
- Human trafficking: this can include forced labor, criminality, organ removal, forced marriage, and prostitution.
- Debt bondage: People trapped who had to borrow money and are forced to work off their debt.
- Slavery of children: the exploitation of children that are forced into prostitution (regardless of the sex), military, criminality, and domestic slavery.

Unfortunately for many people, the concepts of oppression are more concerning than real oppression. Slavery is not a thing of the past; many people benefit from modern-day slavery, which occurs all over the world. By ignoring the actual past and failing to draw any lessons from it, we direct our efforts toward making up for lost ground rather than making progress in the here and now and in the future. Contemporary slavery is genuine, true, and supported by concrete data.

Concerning the "1619 Project," just claiming that it was validated by trustworthy sources without providing specifics on the sources and how that information was processed, if through primary sources and concrete evidence, leaves nothing but suspicion. In other words, saying "I fact checked" just to say "I fact checked" without presenting actual evidence is risky since many people will trust this newly manufactured "truth" above genuine facts because it sounds and feels nicer to your audience or point of view. The idea of starting the history of the United States with slavery in 1619 not only ignores the complete basis of history, slavery, and how the nation was founded, but it also creates a future generation of victimization and bitterness rather than pride. How can I conclude this? This can be seen in history when it comes to revolutions and the individuals who write history after them. Marxism holds that "the history of all hitherto existing society is the history of class struggles"[40], whereas Vladimir Lenin's publications supported demonization, example propaganda, and objectives justify the means[41]. This is why history should be founded on facts rather than feelings of being right, good, or angry. History is about discovering truths based on evidence and learning from those discoveries. Perhaps one day fact will equal truth rather than being opposed to reality.

Questions

1. **Reflect on History:** History has changed over time for the sake of empowering ideals. This is not new. Napoleon Bonaparte, the French self declared emperor in the 18th century who nearly brought Europe to its knees, has stated that "history is a set of lies agreed upon". However, historians have been able to uncover primary credible sources of history to give us facts and truths about the past. What importance is it to understand the truth with facts within your history?
   1. Debate on these topics or write an argument to support your findings.
      1. **TIP:** Always remember to get all sides and NOT just the one that makes you feel good.
2. **Question:** If we only focused on learning negative historical facts on one culture, country, and/or society, describe how a person would most likely feel towards the group. Search online for 2 groups who have no negative historical features and if you can't find them, why do you believe that is the case?
3. **Small Project-Based Practice:** Divide a paper (or notebook) into three parts and do your own research of history that interests you. However, the three parts need to be filled with "Positive", "Negative", and "Neutral". Regardless of how you feel about that particular subject, you must fill in all three categories. After your findings, reflect on your judgments. Did it change? If so, how? If not, did you accept the negative and neutral findings as something you can live with if you were the oppressor/oppressed? (Please see the Case study Morals and Ethics)

Case Study III: History, The Lifeblood of Society

"A generation which ignores history has no past and no future."

–ROBERT HEINLEIN

[During the "summer of love" protests in 2020, I noticed a pattern of rewriting and erasing history. This is not unusual during times of revolution, transformation, or cultural shift. It is critical to understand why this occurs, who benefits, and what possible consequences individuals pursuing change are seeking.]

Common History brings people together to establish social communities. As a result, changing history because of perspectives or special interests is almost a crime. America's history has altered so drastically that it is unrecognizable from what was taught 100 years ago. You'd never guess that our history books once included Hispanic and Black heroes. When someone is proclaimed credible and praised nearly like a king, nothing can stop them from changing history if they so desire. No one in American history has been more infamous for employing this tactic than former President Woodrow Wilson. Wilson was an academic who held a Phd in political science, was the president of Princeton University, had a passion for history, earned Nobel peace prize winner, and was also a known white supremacist[42]. Nonetheless, many respected organizations believe Wilson to be one of the greatest presidents in history[43]. As a case study, let us apply critical thinking methods and historical data to explain the "Wilson effect," which eventually leads to the challenges we face today. Our best place to begin is at the beginning; we must observe Wilson's youth and the political context of the moment.

"Tommy" Woodrow Wilson was the son of a preacher who backed the Confederacy during the Civil War before becoming President of the United States. Wilson grew up as a sympathizer as a result. But, history will show that he despised war. How has this changed over time? The conquerors, after all, write history. The desire to reunite the country during and after the Civil War was so strong that the Republicans (founded as an anti-slavery party) made a concession to get the Democrats back into the fold. Furthermore, Abraham Lincoln chose Democrats as his Vice President for both of his years in office to demonstrate to the people that he is working to re-establish the Union. Now here's something else to think about: Lincoln, contrary to what you may have heard from propaganda or dishonest historians (those who assert a "truth" without providing evidence or primary sources to back up that "truth"), did NOT favor slavery, NEVER held slaves, and Desired equality for ALL[44] despite his one statement during a political debate that suggested otherwise. Additionally, slavery was at the heart of the Civil War. In the "Declaration of the Immediate Causes Which Induce and Justify the Secession of South Carolina from the Federal Union", the mention of the word "slave" is 18 times; Georgia's declaration mentioned the term "slave" 35 times. Mississippi's proclamation mentioned the term "slave" seven times; Texas' declaration mentioned the term "slave" 22 times; and Virginia, despite being a slave-holding state, mentioned the term slave only once (20 times), which they use as the Democratic party's whole defense. This is significant because, following Lincoln's assassination, Democrat Vice President Andrew Johnson became the president. Remember that Johnson was also a southern sympathizer. This hampered the country's progress, which, like Lincoln's legacy, desired equal rights AND opportunities for ALL People.

Johnson took office following Lincoln's unexpected death, which stalled significant progress. Republicans, who now control the House, are the only party capable of stalling the executive branch, but only so much can be accomplished within Congress without the assistance of the executive branch, and vice versa. This is an excellent example of the United States' separation of powers and checks and balances, but I digress. Johnson maintained his anti-abolitionist position and returned enough authority to the Democrats before leaving office[45]. FORMER slave owners from the South were now able to not only begin enforcing horrific local laws known as "Jim Crow" laws, but also to establish the Ku Klux Klan, a domestic terrorist group (KKK). The KKK's intention was to militarily back the Democratic Party while terrorizing and killing blacks and known southern Republicans. The KKK's power grab began with the development of former slaves as an educated and fast force in politics and economics. Consider this: one day you were a slave being beaten and forced to do harsh manual labor, and the next you are free to travel wherever you choose. Consider this: thanks to the 13th Amendment, you can now vote for your next President and local representatives. This was a major concern for the Klan. During election season, the KKK would stand near voting booths with weapons drawn, ensuring that Negroes did not vote. Additionally, if they discovered you were a Republican, regardless of race, you would be forced to leave the line or killed[46]. This use of voting suppression gradually restored Democratic Congressional control, but it had to contend with Republican Presidents Grant, a veteran Union General, who fought the KKK with federal laws, the military, and huge arrests[47]. But, the principle of separation of powers applies both ways, and Grant as president can only do so much. At the next election, blacks and southern Republicans began carrying firearms to ensure their right to vote. As a result, Democrats begin to oppose gun rights. This was the first time the ideas of "gun control" were discussed. Now that you understand the political and ideological framework, let's look at Woodrow Wilson.

President Wilson was dubbed the "Academic President" of the United States. Remember, he was a professor and Princeton University's president. Before his election, he published a series of history books that established the industry standard for history teaching. Trouble with his books, he purposefully excluded practically ALL Blacks and Hispanics while proclaiming a dominance of white race. Illustrations of persons of color in textbooks appeared to be caricatures of a monkey dressed in clothing. Prior to Wilson, historical figures included Lemuel Haynes, Richard Allen, Absalom Jones, Crispus Attucks, and Admiral David Farragut (a Hispanic Admiral in the United States Navy during the Civil War and Grant's "right hand man"). We also had a Black American, Wentworth Cheswell, who was a Patriot during the American Revolution and was chosen as an American assessor, auditor, and Justice of the Peace in New Hampshire beginning in 1768. Furthermore, as a result of this intellectual shift, most Americans today are unaware that, during the American Revolution, there was already a black prominent abolitionist group known as the Free African Society[48] [49] [50]. Prominent Quaker Christians who were instrumental in the abolition of slavery and the education of blacks were also erased from history. Between President Grant and President Teddy Roosevelt, the Klan was declining, and the Black communities held wealth in the south until the election of the "Academic President". If that wasn't enough, he rekindled the Ku Klux Klan (KKK) by showing "The Birth of a Nation," a KKK propaganda film, as the first film shown in the White House. He openly complimented it. Wilson's history books were cited as inspiration by the film's creator. During his presidency, the north and south gradually began to employ various versions of Jim Crow. President Wilson, on the other hand, was well appreciated and praised because of his education, charm, and use of eloquence. He helped establish the rights of women to vote, established the first military occupation (which we now call the "War Machine"), and helped build "The League of Nations" which later became the "United Nations" after World War II [51] [52].

Therefore, why alter history, and how did he benefit a nation? A common history binds a group together to form communities. For example, in ancient Greece, philosophers would congregate to speak and pass on knowledge of the past as well as future thoughts while criticizing the present. Native tribes in the Americas performed similar things. How can two groups of people do similar things but be separated by an ocean? It's just a normal humanistic thing to do. Yet, once you have control over and can change history, you get the ability to manipulate a group. Wilson was a highly renowned academic with clout as Princeton's president. He persuaded academics to teach a new version of history. These academics educate students who will go on to become future leaders and educators. Can you see the sequence of events? With a small group in important places, you can either elevate or lower a certain group. Nazi Germany, an alt-right organization that brought Europe to its knees, burned books, and the far-left Soviet Union, which nearly destroyed the world with nuclear war, forced the collection of books (named Spet-skhran)[53] [54]. Both used propaganda and persuasion to change history. Despite their diametrically opposed viewpoints, they knew that if you dominate knowledge, you control the masses. Could you imagine if, instead of focusing on victims, we taught our youngsters about our nations' heroes, who not only represented diverse races but shared the same values? This is why, as a society, we must conserve history (the good, the bad, and the ugly) and share as much information as possible!

Questions

1. **Reflect on Wilson:** Wilson believed in women's equal rights and also believed people of color were inferior. He changed a common history that different races in America shared and helped end World War I. Based on this knowledge, what is your evaluation of President Wilson? Explain.
    - Debate on these topics or write an argument to support your findings.
        - TIP: Writing argumentative essays and/or having civil debates is an excellent way to expand your critical thinking skills. I advise you to do a quick investigation on facts and truly analyze your arguments by seeking information that supports and opposes president Wilson. You need all perspectives to avoid rhetoric influence from one side over the other.

2. **Question:** If we remove historical figures that have done things we find unethical; how can we learn from unethical actions of the past? Explain your theory.

3. **Small Project-Based Practice:** Find a historical figure that people argue if they are heroic or villainous in our history (or current climate). Great examples would be Christopher Columbus, Abraham Lincoln, Theodore Roosevelt, Hugo Chavez, and Donald Trump. Find arguments from BOTH perspectives (remember, your facts and truths must be aligned). The information you put together would be your case studies. Once you have all your cases and understand both perspectives, create an argument that supports AND opposes the person of study.
    - **TIP:** Your case study for this exercise may be a simple example that is both factual and true. For example: One claim would be that Genocide is evil; a case study would be the former Milosevic regime of the Yugoslav army. During the Kosovo War, Milosevic's army committed around 1.5 million crimes of rape, murder, and kidnappings of Kosovo-Albanian civilians between the years 1998-1999.
    - **NOTE:** The goal of this exercise is to understand that individuals in our history are not as simple as black and white but, like every human, different shades of gray with vast complexities and faults.

Case Study IV: A History Lesson: Socialism against Socialism against Socialism

"The road to hell is paved with good intentions."

—ABBOT BERNARD OF CLAIRVAUX

[I find the socialist ideology fascinating. I say this because the ideas are wonderful in theory, but disastrous in practice, and can only be maintained by the use of force. In addition, disagreements arise from the fact that there are several forms of socialism. Since the ideas of Socialism began, they have devoured one another until only the strongest survived, leading to increasingly autocratic regimes. Despite their ignorance, many seek it out because the ideas behind it sound appealing and humanitarian when, in practice, it is the opposite.]

Depending on who you talk to, there is a distinction between Socialism and Capitalism. I studied the small contrasts between "Democratic Socialism" and "Communist Socialism" as an undergraduate at Queens College (City University of New York). Because Philosophy was my major subject, I was required to read and critically examine the European philosophies of Plato, Karl Marx, Friedrich Nietzsche, Immanuel Kant, Georg Wilhelm Friedrich Hegel, John Stuart Mill, William James, and John Dewey. I was also interested in and studied Asian/Eastern philosophy, including Lao Tzu, Confucius, Buddha, Kokugaku, and Rangaku. Socialism's concepts were well-known to me, and many (but not all) of my teachers, who did not teach me critical thinking or logical techniques, extolled the virtues of Socialism. Unfortunately for those teachers who preached rather than taught, my first and most influential class was "Critical Thinking," taught by a Professor who required us to write papers and explore various issues in depth. We also got bonus points on papers if we employed causality (cause and effect) and identified conditions if certain things were different (probability). Nonetheless, many individuals comprehend the definition of Socialism but do not understand the differences between the many varieties of Socialism.

Socialism is actually both an economic term and a political ideology. It creates an equal distribution and, in most instances, equal outcome. The Merriam-Webster dictionary defines it as[55]:

1. any of various economic and political theories advocating collective or governmental ownership and administration of the means of production and distribution of goods
2. a system of society or group living in which there is no private property
   ◦ a system or condition of society in which the means of production are owned and controlled by the state
3. a stage of society in Marxist theory transitional between capitalism and communism and distinguished by unequal distribution of goods and pay according to work done

This straightforward definition is more complicated than it appears. Socialism comes in a variety of flavors. The main economic distinction between Socialism and Capitalism is that Socialism is concerned with the collective, whilst Capitalism is concerned with individuals. I caution you not to pass judgment on the two if you do not comprehend the statement you just read. Allow me to elaborate, Socialism takes economics and politics a step further. According to the Corporate Finance Institute[56], Here are some of the differences:

- Democratic socialism: In democratic socialism, factors of production are under the management of an elected administration. Vital goods and services such as energy, housing, and transit are distributed through centralized planning, while a free market system is used to distribute consumer products.
- Revolutionary socialism: The running philosophy of revolutionary socialism is that a socialistic system can't emerge while capitalism is still in play. Revolutionaries believe that the road to a purely socialistic system requires a lot of struggle. In such a system, the factors of production are owned and run by workers through a well-developed and centralized structure.
- Libertarian socialism: Works on the assumption that people are always rational, self-determining, and autonomous. If capitalism is taken away, people naturally turn to a socialistic system because it is able to meet their needs.
- Market socialism: The production process is under the control of ordinary workers. The workers decide how resources should be distributed. The workers

sell off what is in excess or give it out to members of the society, who then distribute resources based on a free market system.

- Green socialism: Protective of natural resources. Large corporations in a green socialistic society are owned and run by the public. In addition, green socialism promotes the development and use of public transit, as well as the processing and sale of locally grown food. The production process is focused on ensuring that every member of the community has enough access to basic goods. Moreover, the public is guaranteed a sustainable wage[57].

These forms of economic phrases are part of a "Planned Economy". Consider how a civilization debated and "planned" to generate goods or services for its people. There are many more words for Socialism, but some of the benefits, in theory, are that each worker in the community gets a say in how the resources are managed, and it makes the best use of the employees' skills. However, the greatest disadvantage of Socialism (and this would be key in our examples) is dependency on cooperation within the community and lack of competitiveness and innovation. In other words, individual trust and motivation. The ideology of Socialism can have the same benefits and drawbacks.

Socialism ideology can be very different based on who you ask. Socialism began with "Utopian Socialism" by Robert Owen, Henri de Saint-Simon, and Charles Fourier who influenced Karl Marx, the creator of the popular "Marxism". Around the same time of the rise of Marx came Communism, which believes in socio-economic structured ideas for common ownership thanks to a classless and stateless social organization[58]. Many have argued that socialism is not Communism but it was Lenin who declared that "the goal of socialism is Communism " (we will dive into Lenin in a moment). Maoism, founded by Mao Zedong, held that class conflict is always present in society and that one must be watchful. "Political power comes from the barrel of the gun," Mao said. Autonomism is a subset of Socialism and Marxism that emphasizes self-organized activity outside of existing organizational structures rather than party political organization. Workers, in other words, are autonomists who promote workplace socialization and slow working conditions. The emphasis is on the antagonism of capitalism rather than on productivity. The most romanticized type of socialism is anarchism. Anarchist socialists support stateless societies. They believe that the concept of "state" is destructive and undesirable to people[59] [60]. This system of government (ironically, because they do not believe in the "state") was tested during the Spanish Civil War at the close of the nineteenth and beginning of the twentieth centuries. In Russia, anarchist socialists supported and participated in the Communist Bolshevik revolution. But, the Bolsheviks soon turned against them. This resulted in the Kronstadt revolt in 1921. Several survivors made their way to Ukraine. After being betrayed by the Bolsheviks, the Anarchists continued to battle the "Whites" (revolutionary opponents). Numerous attempts have been made in Europe at various times but have never taken root. Likewise, during the June 2020 protests in the United States, demonstrators established an area of Seattle Washington as a "Capital Hill Autonomous Zone," also known as CHAZ, which eventually became "Capital Hill Organized Protest" (CHOP) due to (more irony) legality. There are various types of anarchists who combine other characteristics but do not always agree with one another. The following are the items on the list: Mutualism, Collectivist anarchism, Anarcho-communism, Anarcho-syndicalism, and Individualist anarchism are all forms of anarchism.

Democratic Socialism, on the other hand, has received extensive attention in the Western hemisphere. It has an extremely broad connotation that varies depending on who hears it. This data was abundant throughout political debates between 2016 and 2020. Representatives like Alexandria Ocasio-Cortez and Senator Bernie Sanders are both professed Democratic Socialists, but their ideas of what that means are vastly different. The more centrist idea is a mixed economy, which is a hybrid of a planned economy and a free market. They were likewise committed to the concepts of wealth and power redistribution. Yet, the more "left" Democratic Socialists there are, the more they support a socialist society via revolutionary or evolutionary, sometimes known as reform, means (Karl Marx's view of Capitalism being the first step to socialism). There are various interpretations of Democratic Socialism, and many believe that it has never been done before. Hugo Chávez of Venezuela was the first professed Democratic Socialist to achieve success in South America. Unfortunately for the Venezuelan people, it turned out to be a tragedy. Within 20 years, the most privileged country in South America has devolved into one of the poorest and most regulated. Chávez and his "Bolivarian Revolution" redistributed money as promised[61], resulting in the demise of the middle and upper classes who owned enterprises and accounted for the majority of production. The poorer classes did experience some prosperity[62], but only until the funds ran out[63]. Venezuela is now led by "President" Nicolás Maduro, who lost an election but declared it rigged and remained in power. My mother's side of the family has relatives in Venezuela now who are subject to Maduro's policies. Many believe that he took over for Chávez after his death, but they forget that Chávez selected Maduro to several critical positions of power. According to the Wall Street Journal, he is the "most capable administrator and politician in Chávez's inner circle"[64]. There are many more types of socialism, such as Libertarian socialism, Eco-socialism, and Liberal socialism, but for the sake of brevity, let's stick to the hazards of not fully knowing what you don't fully accept.

Misinformation on college campuses, in the media, and in politics today is the result of a lack of understanding. Most people's heads would figuratively burst if I told them the Nazi party was created as a version of Socialism. The acronym

NAZI stands for "Nationalsozialistische" Deutsche Arbeiterpartei (NSDAP), which translates as National-Socialist German Workers' Party in English. Yep, you read that accurately. The Nazi party promoted itself as a Socialist party. Once reviled and prohibited in Germany for years prior to its authority, this kind of National Socialism gained popularity from the 1920s through the 1940s (Hitler was arrested for an attempted coup to overthrow the government). Hitler was never elected in the 1932 election, but due to his popularity, the president of the German republic, Paul von Hindenburg, appointed him chancellor in January 1933. Because of the "burning of the Reichstag," Hitler was granted emergency powers, which gave the Nazis the power they have today[65]. Its Socialism and rage against a "unjustified system" were the catalysts for the totalitarian nation that ignited World War II. Yet, Hitler and the Nazi party required the assistance of huge corporations, which defeated the concepts of Socialism and is why historians do not consider them Socialist[66]. This Alternative "Right" movement resulted in the death of millions of Jews since they were portrayed as a "evil race" by the propaganda. We now know that major corporations joined this effort and provided financial or product assistance to the Nazi party. Nestlé[67], Bayer[68], Barclays Bank[69], Deutsche Bank[70], Chase National Bank (now JP Morgan Chase)[71], IBM[72], BMW[73], Hugo Boss[74], Mercedes-Benz, Porsche, and Volkswagen Group are among these corporations[75]. Unfortunately, this history is being replicated now, with major corporations lowering their ethics in order to gain access to Communist countries known for unethical forced labor.

In contrast, the Soviet Union used Communism rather than Nationalism. This type of Socialism leaned on Karl Marx (a German) and his "Communist Manifesto" to influence Vladimir Lenin and gain his support. Lenin was hardly the only revolutionary who triumphed. But why did Russia's former Czars stage a revolution that resulted in the Soviet Union? The obvious response was poverty. Russia was one of the poorest countries in the early 1900s. Denmark industrialized later than the rest of Europe, but the end of World War I marked the beginning of the end for the royal family. Following Lenin's return from exile, the "October Revolution" erupted, resulting in the founding of the "Bolshevik establishment of the Soviet Union," also known as The Soviet Union[76]. What happened soon after gaining control that would lead to a catastrophe in the millions rivaling the Nazi party. Roughly half a year into their rule, the Bolsheviks developed a secret police to secure their revolution by weeding out, executing, or punishing those thought to be "enemies of the people". This policy was known historically as the Red Terror. This was a significant fire that sparked a Civil War between the Bolsheviks (Reds) and the counter-revolutionaries (Whites). Despite the fact that the Civil War killed and injured millions of people, regardless of whose side you were on, the "Red Army" triumphed, but the "enemy of the people" remained a threat to the party. Lenin's Bolsheviks instituted trials against "enemies of the people" and killed the tzar and the Romanov dynasty. Furthermore, the newly formed Communist Party began indoctrination and cultural revolution by employing various symbols, such as the hammer and sickle with a red background symbolizing the October Revolution, the prohibition of ALL religions and the persecution of the Russian Orthodox Church, and the development of communist messianism (the depiction of Communist leaders as religious figures)[77] [78] [79]. Lenin not only devised these measures, but also elevated Joseph Stalin to positions of power. Several historians claim that Stalin was not a true socialist, but rather a power freak. Prior to his death, Lenin expressed dissatisfaction with Stalin's policies. Yet, Lenin did not depose him, and after his death, Stalin took over and executed all of his opponents in order to cement his reign[80]. Millions of people died between Lenin and Stalin in order to create an equitable distribution of riches. The Gulag archipelago, which originated with Lenin's ideals, established a severe forced labor camp system to purge any political "enemies of the state"[81]. This also provided the Soviet Union with a fresh source of labor. It is unknown how many people died as a result of the Red Terror (1918-1922 by Lenin and Trotsky), the Great Terror, also known as the Great Purge (1936-1938 by Stalin), the Gulags, and the famine that followed redistribution, although the figure is in the tens of millions[82] [83] [84].

The Chinese revolution followed a similar path to the Soviet Union, although the dead toll was closer to 65 million. Because the Chinese Communist regime is still in power, gathering evidence is more difficult than it was in the Soviet Union, which fell in 1992. Despite the fact that the political party is a small organization, they elect a leader to dominate. Many communist systems choose their officials from a pool of communist party members. In the end, even if it is a democratic system, you choose who the party wishes to lead. But what about a different kind of Socialism?

For years, American Democratic Socialists have admired the Nordic model. Sweden was one country that tried Socialism without a revolution or progress. Sweden's Union Institutions had a huge political effect prior to World War II, which finally led to greater Socialist politics, ironically named Social Democrats. Sweden, like the other Nordic countries, began to experience economic deterioration in the early 1980s. The welfare state, in particular, was in serious decline, and changes were required. The first was socializing industrial ownership, while the second was accepting private capital. Finally, the economic crisis was resolved in the 1990s by lowering government spending, deregulating the economy, and privatizing public services. They evolved into capitalists[85] [86]. Sweden has a 74.9 grade on the capitalist scale as of August 2020, whereas the United States has a 76.6. In economic ideology, Sweden is more aligned with the United States[87]. Switzerland, which ranks 82 on the economic freedom scale and is thus more capitalist than the United States, is an honorable mention of a country that is incorrectly characterized as a democratic socialist[88]. Capitalism, which is associated with evil in academia, is a free market system. In short, the power of commodities and services is given directly by the desire of those eager to purchase them. Private ownership and production are common. Individuals must select what is in demand and what is available. Prices are determined by the laws of supply and demand. Many people feel upset with Capitalism at this point. Certain items are not affordable to everyone. Furthermore, many capitalists have created "Monopolies" in which they control not only supply but also prices and the degree of entry to compete. This is the complexity that many have argued about since Capitalism's inception. To its credit, the United States has enacted legislation prohibiting this practice, although some contend that it is insufficient. Also, depending on the company, the treatment of labor has received different reviews. For example, when Microsoft first became a publicly traded firm, it gave its employees shares, often known as stocks, as a bonus. This move not only provided investable interests in the company, but also made ten thousand of its initial employees wealthy[89]. Tesla Motors did something similar to Microsoft, and the results are promising as of this writing.

So, what can we learn from history? What does academia teach about Socialism? Many young people profess to be socialists, but few can answer the question of what kind of socialist they are, let alone grasp what they are proposing. It's also not their fault. Kids are not taught the deadly history of what it takes to keep Socialism in place. Socialism necessitates complete trust in the collective. However, depending on the sort of socialist you are, you may have disagreements with other types of socialists, which can result in bloodshed or being exploited for another purpose (as we saw in our examples earlier). Can you confidently state that you trust everyone in your community and country to do as well as you would with the same exact ethics? High school pupils in Russia are required to read and analyze Aleksandr Solzhenitsyn's The Gulag Archipelago[90]. The reason is to teach their children about their country's sad history. Something we should embrace rather than strive to erase or forget. Socialism, even if imposed with good intentions, invariably results in bloodshed. It begs the question, at what expense do you intend to experiment? If your response is "it has never been tried before," you haven't been paying attention and you probably think you know better than Marx, Lenin, or Mao. Perhaps the solution lies somewhere in the middle (mixed economy).Or maybe the answer is found in an unspecified 1970's Moscow joke: *"What would happen if the Communists occupied the Sahara? Answer: Nothing—for 50 years. Then there would be a shortage of sand"*. My personal belief resonates more with, Lebanese-American Scholar, Nassim Nicholas Taleb in which he wrote in **Skin in the game**, *"I am, at the Fed level, libertarian; at the state level, Republican; at the local level, Democrat; and at the family and friends level, a socialist. If that saying doesn't convince you of the fatuousness of left vs. right labels, nothing will"*[91].

Questions

1. **Reflect on Socialism:** Socialism is one of the biggest discussions within the academic community despite having a terrible historical outcome. Fictional novels have had several examples of utopias and dystopias around socialism that were both disturbing and heart breaking. Nevertheless, 40% of Americans believe in some form of Socialism.
   - Write down or discuss why socialism is such an enticing form of government and why, despite the belief of it being positive, it always ends with poverty and death.
2. **Question:** Explain why you think people continue to argue that socialism "wasn't done right". Why do you think western education does not teach the history of socialism and communism but will teach the horrors of the Nazi party?
   - **TIP:** Try to look for evidence that supports your claim. Do not just assume. Try to use proper logic in your decision.
3. **Small Project-Based Practice:** What is your "Utopia"? Create its economic, social, and political structure. How is healthcare managed? How are taxes accessed? How are the defenses, intelligence, education, arts, and businesses created and maintained? Once all this is done, how would you manage inflation, deflation, international affairs with other countries with different moral values than yours? How would you manage civil unrest if it was (and like all civilizations, will) to occur? How are judges and laws created?
   - **NOTE:** This is one of the most difficult assignments if you take the time to actually do it correctly. This also requires a significant amount of research. Many political leaders can't answer half of these questions correctly without thinking of repercussions and yet can get reelected by simply sounding educated and having a personality that you like. Therefore, have fun with this project and use critical thinking strategies.

Case Study V: News Media/ Social Media of the Early 21st Century: Some Truths and No Facts Gets You Clicks

"The media's the most powerful entity on earth. They have the power to make the innocent guilty and to make the guilty innocent, and that's power. Because they control the minds of the masses."

–MALCOLM X

[I noticed a particular pattern in gaslighting, misinformation, disinformation, and misleading "fact-checks" based on semantics while watching and reading corporate news. Numerous people on social media were duped by truths that were not supported by facts. When someone exposes the lies, their personalities are attacked rather than the argument. This essay illuminates the situation.]

A natural phenomena has occurred since the invention of the printing press. The ability to spread a message to the masses with minimal effort. Prior to it, people will teach the public through telling stories, shouting in town halls or city centers, and/ or using lecture tactics. When the printing press was established, it became easier not only to convey your message, but also to further elaborate your arguments in a more orderly manner. The printing press was unquestionably a critical component to the growth of the American Revolution in the Colonies of America (before the United States). Imagine, you turn to your chosen news outlet and you read the headline "Boston Massacre, Five people killed by soldiers!". This would elicit an outcry and stir your emotions. And the Boston Gazette reported it on March 5th, 1770. This information spread like wildfire throughout the 13 colonies[92]. This is what we would term "trending" today. I should highlight that one of the first Americans killed in that massacre was a black man named Crispus Attucks, for whom the country mourned his death during the period when slavery was still legal[93]. But when did people's opinions become news? One could claim that it began in the United States with the 1800 election. Federalist John Adams against Democratic-Republican Thomas Jefferson (not to be mistaken for the political parties today). During the election, the former allies became bitter opponents, resulting in a bi-partisan political fight akin to what we see today. John Adams was one of the first to mention Jefferson's connection with Sally Hemmings, Jefferson's household slave at the time, and claimed he was a "a mean-spirited, low-lived creature". Jefferson's supporters accused Adams of being a "hideous hermaphrodite" who sought to spark a war with France[94]. This is referred to as "false news" nowadays. This election established the precedent for partisan newspapers and media outlets in the United States. The first amendment guarantees free speech, but it does not guarantee all speech[95]. It brings me to the media of the twenty-first century.

"Clicks" on social media produce advertising money. If you go to your favorite YouTube channel and see an advertisement for a political campaign, video game, or new stock strategy, you have contributed to the advertiser's payment to not only the author of the video, but also to Youtube itself. Each click prompts the advertiser to pay. The same may be stated when you click on any Amazon sponsor when searching for an item online. All of your behaviors are collected and can be used to assess your interests and the likelihood of you "clicking" on the advertisement. It is beneficial to the social media hosts, the company/organization marketing the item/concept, and you gain the mental joy of looking at the product/idea and potentially purchasing or adopting that thing or idea as a result of the algorithm[96]. Numerous businesses have been accused of selling information to their clients, and social media is no exception. They have sold and researched in order to predict the actions or probability of the people. And the employment of rhetoric has been a driving force of human behavior and the news because as we connect more with one another, we expose our own views, thoughts, and desires to the algorithm. As a result, "click baits" proliferated. In the political realm, during President Donald J. Trump's impeachment, the phrases "Trump" and "Russia" were among the most popular online trends for months. The news organizations were one of the leaders that benefited from this. It is no longer a secret that social media and the internet are the primary sources of information in the twenty-first century. And, as social media and the internet become the major sources of information, large news channels begin to lose readership, which correlates to a loss of ad revenue. Furthermore, the mix of political party agendas and the competitiveness of increasingly independent web outlets results in a new approach of generating news for the masses.

Nothing could be more common than the 2020 quarantine pandemic. When a country is quarantined due to a pandemic, you begin to rely on social media and web access more than ever before. Like many other teachers, I was forced to switch my in-person classroom to an online-only environment. Students privately expressed personal concerns about the rise in social media bullying and misleading information spreading faster than ever before (and these are children from ages 12-14). Most adults may not have noticed because of other fear factors, but teenagers in these times did. The misinterpretation of facts to declare them true has clearly driven a society that previously encouraged variety and unity. In June 2020, for example, my wife and I witnessed a live video stream of riots and looting on Manhattan's 34th street (near "Manhattan Mall" and Penn Station). The following day, New York City Mayor Bill De Blasio pronounced it "largely peaceful"[97]. I'm not sure what the definition of most peaceful is, but witnessing two people fight and steal another person's stolen Apple computer product doesn't seem to suit. CNN, CBS, and MSNBC have claimed that federal agents protecting federal buildings and arresting "peaceful protestors" while attempting to destroy the building is an "insurgency," despite the fact that those buildings house records of convicted criminals, victims, and private information of individuals. Furthermore, the federal government, not the state, has control over federal structures. This is analogous to embassies; a foreign government is accountable for its embassies within the foreign country in which they are located (example: if you enter a British Embassy in New York, you are no longer in United States jurisdiction). Consider this: if you're on social media and see a story that says "Federal Forces strike peaceful protestors," the chances of you or someone you know clicking on it are quite high. Regardless of whether you believe the story is "fake news" or not, you have provided them with the advertising click they required to maintain their operation.

It is not our fault as humans to want to click on bogus news headlines or read newspapers that promote our personal preferences. To the greatest extent possible, we are emotional beings. We react emotionally to pictures before we attempt to understand them logically[98]. That is also how we disrupt our surroundings. But, one of the things that distinguishes us from the animals is our ability to reason and critically think. The ability to employ logic is one significant factor that distinguishes individuals from the masses. We must remember to employ these skills when determining facts and truths. Social media platforms, news sources, and organizations are all aware of and capable of utilizing these methods to their advantage. Even non-profit companies (which can keep a large portion of their profits)[99] [100] employ strategic language and click bait methods to attract attention. Propaganda is another term for fake news. How is this true? Thanks to Dictionary.com, here is the following definitions[101] [102]:

- Fake News: false news stories, often of a sensational nature, created to be widely shared or distributed for the purpose of generating revenue, or promoting or discrediting a public figure, political movement, company, etc.

- Propaganda: information, ideas, or rumors deliberately spread widely to help or harm a person, group, movement, institution, nation, etc.; the deliberate spreading of such information, rumors, etc.

As a result, it is up to you to decide what news you will accept and believe. Before making a proper judgment, listen to/read the true facts rather than the highlights of edited and interpreted material.

Questions

1. **Reflect on Media:** Examine what gets you to click on a headline. Is the rhetoric triggering you to click on that headline or pick up that newspaper? Reflect on one headline you believed to be the news and when you were done understanding the article, realized it wasn't exactly what the headline suggested.
   1. This is a great opportunity to discuss this with someone or record your voice reflecting on what you felt before and after you read/heard the entire news article.
2. **Question:** In a country like the United States that holds the first Amendment to be a vital constitutional right (Freedom of: Speech, Press, Religion, Assembly), should the country have laws that restrict the media from displaying false or unproven claims? If so/not, explain why? Compare and contrast the pros and cons for limiting the press.
   1. TIP: Find evidence from other countries who do not have a commercial news media and see their outcomes. I can say from experience, it has very mixed results. This is simply an exercise on your critical thinking skills, there is know right or wrong answer.
3. **Small Project-Based Practice:** Watch/Read a news article that is left leaning (such as CNN, MSNBC, or PBS) and write down what the headline was and the highlighted use of rhetoric
   1. Now watch/read the same topic on a more right leaning outlet (such as FOX, Daily Wire) and repeat the process of documentation.
   2. Find the source of both news outlets and watch/read the source in its entirety.
   3. Examine the results: compare and contrast your findings from the different news outlets and the main source.
   4. Create your own news article on the same topic that is neutral. Remember to have all the facts and avoid using left or right leaning rhetoric. The examples you have from step 1 and 2 would be your reference.
   5. After you are done, analyze your news article: Is your news article more informed than the other outlets? If you were to try to get advertising

revenue, do you believe that you would spark more emotional clicks or less by not using sensational headlines?

Case Study VI: The ideology of the 20th century educational system and the effects today

"Communism counts its opportunities in terms of decades - not of weeks. Its means of aggression consist not only of nuclear weapons and missiles with enormous boosters, and not only of spies, agents and terrorists, but of great masses of men and women, deluded by a common ideology which inspires them with a false hope."

—ROBERT KENNEDY

[With promotions of different ideologies that may be counterproductive to what we want our children to learn, I felt it was vital to highlight how the educational system became what it is today.]

As a teacher, I am essentially in a lion's den; most teachers and academics believe in a certain ideology to the point of religion, and if you disagree, you will be eaten alive. The educational system has been increasingly split since former President Wilson published "A History of the American People" (the truth can be determined by analyzing the use of rhetoric that President Wilson used in his books). Minorities were no longer learning their true history, and racial divisions became rampant. Things didn't start to change until the civil rights movement, and "Black History Month" was established in 1976[103]. You are obligated or "highly encouraged" to teach all about blackness and its history for one month out of an entire calendar year. But why only for one month? In reality, there should be no Black or Hispanic history month because America is a colorful country with a rich DIVERSE history, which should be emphasized. Many people are unaware that an openly gay man named Baron Friedrich von Steuben was one of the creators of the professional United States armed force. Despite being a homosexual, George Washington not only revered and appreciated Steuben, but he was also granted citizenship, land, and lived openly with the renowned John Mulligan after the war[104]. Transgender people, Blacks, Indigenous, Hispanics, Asians, and Women have all played important roles in American history. I feel that if a history teacher actually cared about the worth of a rich past rather than ideology, our kids would have a different perspective on America. And therein lies the difficulty in today's educational system, which is a direct outcome of the twentieth century. As a culture, we have prioritized ideology, social justice beliefs, and critical theory. Schools have likewise embraced the concept of equality vs equity without contemplating the potential consequences of one over the other or the fact not everything needs to be equitable or equal all the time. Most educators are quite humanistic, so I don't blame them. They don't do it for the money or the glory because, to be honest, educators get very little of either. So, what is the problem with the educational system? We can examine the history of the twentieth century and conclude that it was a combination of changing history for the sake of influence, living through one of the bloodiest centuries in written history, and the cold war nearly destroying the planet, or we can examine how ideology and morals changed, resulting in a chain of events that eventually led to the educational system we see today. I'll go with the latter for this case study because it's more complicated than you might think.

Try to picture this: The sky is overcast, as it usually is on a morning. Contrary to popular belief, however, humans are responsible for the gloomy gray sky we see today. The birds have stopped singing, and the fresh bread fragrance has faded. In its stead, a thick cloud of factory smoke with the deafening noises of hammering, screams, and the whirring of machinery. When you leave your modest home, which is made primarily of ancient bricks and wood, you spot a child racing past you. The kid without shoes is not rushing to make it to class on time. He was late for work, so he had to hurry. We now find ourselves in the midst of the nineteenth-century industrial revolution. There have been worse times for capitalism than this. Child labor and salaries were not regulated. The lack of available farmland or the inability to keep up with market demands and pricing forced many people to seek employment in industries instead. Although it began in England, the industrial revolution quickly spread to the Americas and beyond[105]. As a result, many artists, including writers, teachers, politicians, and philosophers, took action in their respective disciplines. Thus, the "Progressive Period" came into being.

Despite the fact that the majority of the nineteenth century saw the greatest spread of the industrial revolution, the "Progressive Period" rejected the ideas of cruel conditions from the industrial revolution. Furthermore, with slavery abolished in the United States, a fresh round of "reconstruction" was required. Although the "Progressive Era" was where they handled these issues, it was not until the birth of the twentieth century that we fully see ideas put into practice. The Frankfurt School was founded around this time. This school's goal was to delve deeply into social theory and critical philosophy. The Frankfurt School pupils, like many philosophers of the nineteenth century, believed in a type of social justice (no pun intended) for the working class. Furthermore, they believed that capitalism was a necessary step toward socialism and the birth of Utopia. These ideas spread quickly, and several political philosophies emerged. Those who did not participate in politics, on the other hand, chose to further evaluate their philosophy through study.

Prior to the development of the Nazi party and the closure of the Frankfurt school, which resulted in a large number of refugees fleeing to the United States and France, the "Red Scare" posed the greatest threat to capitalist countries. This "Red Scare" resulted in widespread injustice for persons who were even accused of being Communists. This engendered hostility toward people who were not avowed communists but simply believed in equal rights for all[106]. As Nazi Germany fell, the pioneers of critical theory took significant posts in universities, where they taught their theories, conducted research with graduating students, and finally returned to the Frankfurt School. Their impact, however, lives on via their pupils and those who lived through the Great Depression firsthand. It was almost too simple to dislike capitalism. Several former KGB Soviet Union operatives defected to the United States in the mid-20th century, informing the western world about the dangers of socialism and what, at the time, the Soviet Union had become (more on this later).

Many students during the Civil Rights era were offspring of Industrial Revolution thought. The critical theory merely shifted the moral compass from economics to race, gender, and culture as a whole. As we stated in the last chapter, the theory is appealing, and any humanist can almost agree with the views that critical theorists hold. That is the rationale of our current educational system. Several of those students who were socialism-trained grew up and pursued careers in various fields. Many people who desire to contribute to societal development pursue education in order to educate future generations. As I previously stated, very few, if any, people go into teaching for the sake of money or glory. They wish to motivate and educate others. The problem is that many academics who trained future educators in the mid-to-late twentieth century believed in progressivism and socialism as a result of the principles they absorbed as students at the University. Not on genuine life experience, but on teachings given by the preceding generation of Professors, i.e. the Frankfurt School immigrants. Let's examine further:

• Assume four critical theory professors teach in one semester a combined total of 320 students (80 students for each professor or 4 classes with about 20 students).

- To be very conservative with the number; out of 320 students, 16 are influenced and indoctrinated (ratio 20:1 or for every class of 20 students, 1 student is sold on the idea of whichever subject within the critical theory)
- Out of the 16, 4 become educators within one year (assuming they are college seniors).
- Now we have a total of 8 professors teaching the subject in one semester a combined total of 640 students (same amount of students per class)
- Repeat this process for 100 years.

This is entirely theoretical and not a social science study, so I will not claim this example as truth and it should be researched further, but that does not negate the fact that teachers have an influence on their students. I've personally witnessed this when a few students approached me and told me how I motivated them to become lawyers, politicians, and other remarkable occupations in social science. This pushed me to keep working, which I believe is the same drive that other instructors experience when they receive similar feedback from their kids. This leads to the education system in the twenty-first century.

The issue with education now is when we start teaching what to think rather than HOW to think. Imagine studying in social studies that you are a victim of an oppressed society rather than learning HOW society works and how you may operate within it (which eventually can lead to change that YOU would like to see). The topic itself becomes about victims against oppressors. We are also taught to elevate specific ethnicities and sexual orientations without contemplating the long-term consequences that history has shown us. What is more terrible is that, after nearly two generations of this style of education, I believe many of our present educators are unaware that this type of teaching can have disastrous consequences in Western civilization. We teach racism, sexism, and sexuality/gender norms to children in preoperational stages (ages 2-7), when their brains are still struggling to learn proper syntax and grammar and complicated abstract thinking is still very difficult[107]. If you still have any doubt, analyze this:

> When doing anything in the classroom, teachers are "encouraged" to read academic research publications on education. If you wish to change a strategy, you must use tried and true methods. But, in order for a professor to be published and recognized by other educators, it must be authorized by the journal's editorial board. James Lindsay, Helen Pluckrose, and Peter Boghossian, three professors, tested a notion about how critical theory is taking over the

educational system. To test the notion, they published 20 phony papers filled with trendy lingo. Furthermore, the academics took Adolf Hitler's manifesto *"Mein Kampf"* and replaced the keywords with feminist jargon rather than words like "Germans" and "Jews" when outlining what needed to be done about patriarchy. Bear in mind that the framework of *"Mein Kampf"* changed very little. These were not only published, but also attracted considerable interest. Who knows what instructors might have proposed to pupils if this complex scam had not been exposed as a hoax[108] [109].

We as a culture have forgotten the core reasons why schools were established in the first place. Schools were established in various societies to produce good citizens, Christians/Jews/Muslims, or warriors (of course it all depends on the culture within that society). Yet, it ultimately boils down to one thing: producing excellent people for their society. To be a good member of society in a republic, however, one needs to know HOW to think rather than WHAT to believe. As a result, if we continue down the route of teaching future citizens what to think, we will not be far from moral policing and a socialist society in which individuality is not only undesirable but also unacceptable.

Questions

1. **Research on Education:** Search for different schools in different areas of the world (China, Japan, South Korea, etc.). Compare and contrast their education practice (praxis) with the United States/Canada.
    1. Research the culture of the country you choose compared to the United States/Canada. Compare and contrast.
2. After you compare and contrast, what takeaways did you get from that research?
3. How has their culture influenced their educational system?

Case Study VII: The Death of The First Amendment, The Rise of Cancel Culture, and The Intellectual Dark Web

"Propaganda tries to force a doctrine on the whole people... Propaganda works on the general public from the standpoint of an idea and makes them ripe for the victory of this idea".

—ADOLPH HITLER IN MEIN KAMPF

[Originally written with the worry that silenced voices, no matter how ludacris they appear, may be detrimental in the long run. Individuals who speak in public should be challenged because it is the greatest way to put their theories to the test. History has already demonstrated what occurs when you try to compel someone to remain silent.]

During this election, we are in a wild period, and what makes things even more unpredictable is the direction that the United States is taking, with elected people working on developing a database of their political rival's followers. Worse, these are the same folks that allow certain groups to engage in mobs of violence unchallenged. This is an equivalent tactic from those who took part in the French, Russian, and Chinese revolutions.

The first amendment is one of the most beloved Bill of Rights Amendments in the United States. In this amendment, it states the following: "Congress shall make no law respecting an establishment of religion, or prohibiting the free exercise thereof (expression); or abridging the freedom of speech, or of the press; or the right of the people peaceably to assemble, and to petition the Government for a redress of grievances"[110]. Numerous countries have similar rights, but until the twenty-first century, no country has been more vigorous in safeguarding those rights than the United States. Unlike the United States, many countries who have "free speech" laws have implemented legislation to some degree regulating freedom of expression when it comes to "Hate Speech". Despite this, several large commercial companies have begun implementing policies on "Hate speech" and terminating workers or removing people from platforms who are deemed to be guilty of hate speech. This is referred to as what is known as a "canceled".

Americans have become so terrified of stating their minds and getting "canceled" that a Cato Institute poll conducted in July 2020 found that 62% of the US populace is unable to disclose their political ideas[111]. As a result of this pressure, many critical thinkers, social/political activists, religious groups, and even racist organizations have turned to the "black web" to continue their debates, conversations, and perhaps organizational activities. Meanwhile, the United States has made no legal changes regarding free speech, despite the fact that many congressional leaders have made this a significant talking point for private organizations to control the ultimate outcome. This unusual shift in political tactics has produced a power vacuum in terms of who can influence legislation without enacting a single piece of legislation.

So what precisely is "hate speech," how does cancel culture function, and how can the "intellectual dark web" become a safe haven or a source of rebellion? Many groups interpret "hate" words differently. Depending on who you ask, it could be as simple as a kind of communication that displays hatred or urges violence against a certain individual or group based on their identity, and we have laws that protect people who incite violence. What is more complicated, and currently the most debated, is a style of communication that expresses disdain or enmity for a certain person or group based on race, color, sexual orientation, gender, handicap, or nationality. In other words, hate speech occurs when you speak or appear to express something unpleasant about a specific group. In these circumstances, it would be quite easy for an argument about moral values, race, politics, and culture to devolve fast into a hate speech claim, which would immediately halt the conversation and devolve into anarchy.

Many young people are taught that giving the opposing opinion a chance to speak encourages hate speech. This is taught as part of Critical Theory courses in our educational system. Studies and theories, like most concepts, originate at the university level before reaching primary schools. The first of many college campuses to experience this was Evergreen University, which had a riot in 2017.

Prior to the Evergreen University riots, several universities had been relatively progressive. A Call to Action forum on anti-racism began on October 28th, 2015. After attending an anti-racism summit, lecturers began to announce a list of steps that needed to be taken. The knowledge circulated among students, and on November 16th, 2016, the council devised a plan to combat racism and equity concerns in The Canoe Meeting. Sadly, they did not identify a single reference to the concerns, although claiming to have a problem. This is analogous to a doctor informing a patient that they are ill without first meeting the patient. According to Dr. Bret Weinstein (PhD), a former professor, he recognized the problem at these seminars and expressed his concerns loudly. Students and faculty members began to oppose racism and white supremacy more vocally. Later, during a faculty meeting, he was accused of racism, and when attempting to defend himself, he was told he couldn't since it would be racist to do so. Students began to take control of the university, and they were praised for their activities every time they stopped a lecture or presentation. This encouragement finally led to the 2017 riot. Students and faculty were invited to take a day off to recognize the power of race. People would be absent on "Day of Absence" based on their race. It was the Caucasians' turn to be absent that day this year. Weinstein refused to protest since it was a public college and he had the right to be there.

This sparked widespread calls for his resignation. When university police arrived to protect Weinstein, they were accused of racism. Following that, the protest organizers met with the top administrators. Protesters also claimed that Weinstein teaches science, and that STEM is inherently racist. The cafeteria gathering later that year was a watershed moment in the demonstrations. Seats in the front and food were given for persons of color only and any person of color that defended Weinstein were labeled "anti-black". When students had not received Weinstein's resignation, they began barricading the library, which was also the administration building, with the administrators inside the following day. In other terms, the academic members were imprisoned. To prevent further inspection, faculty members began to join their captors while imprisoned. Although the president of the University ordered police to stand down, students began to take over the roadways around campus. Rioters began looking for Weinstein. Finally, Weinstein was forced to retire and became one of the pioneers of the "intellectual dark web". The rioters declared triumph as a result of the authorities side with those who imprisoned them. This anarchist strategy later manifested itself in the 2020 riots, as hostility toward hate speech grew across the country.

Although this is an extreme example, many young adults who attended universities went on to professions in municipal politics, law, and technology. Most tech businesses hire fresh out of college with no real-world experience, keeping them in the same group they were in during their studies. It's no surprise that "cultural cancellation" started about this period. This term was coined the same year as the

Evergreen riots, and it refers to the removal of bad actors from their professions, social media accounts, and/or sources of revenue due to inappropriate rhetoric or action. According to the accuser, this type of moral policing is successful in combating harm to others and holding them accountable. To avoid being canceled, one must have the same moral ideals and ideas as the accusers who are feeling oppressed. Moreover, the persons that define the phrases are in a position of power within consulting organizations that specialize in critical theory, social media outlets, or programing corporations that construct Artificial Intelligence algorithms that automatically determine the terminology of a "hate speech". Numerous people, including Congresswoman Tulsi Gabbard, were "canceled" in various ways, claiming either hate speech or violating terms of agreement without specifying which provisions were violated. Congress has summoned the CEOs of big technology corporations on several occasions, with little to no success. "Cancel culture" is still alive and thriving as of this writing. As a result, the "intellectual dark web" emerges.

The "Intellectual Dark Web" is popular among many people. People and groups have begun to develop their own communication channels and social media platforms. Eric Weinstein (PhD), Bret Weinstein's brother, was the first to develop this word. Eric (not to be confused with Bret, I shall refer to first names moving forward) compared figuratively to the opposition of mainstream media, which at the time pushed numerous sorts of "cancel culture". Conservative and classical liberal celebrities came together to continue conversations about identity politics, political correctness, partisan politics, education, and, of course, cancel culture. Conversations about these problems, ironically, might be "canceled" if an opposing argument is permitted to speak on their behalf. The nature of the Intellectual Dark Web grew more difficult to identify as this sort of "underground" communication evolved. Several people use the word to describe online debates on unpopular or less controlled venues about postmodernism, Marxism, tribalism, and free speech. Additional irony and historical data reveals that people who genuinely do the typical hate speech and are pushed into hiding unite others who have been disenfranchised by various societal situations.

The Nazi party and the Bolsheviks were the two most popular and well-documented organizations that were forced into the shadows yet eventually rose to power. Both groups were unpopular and were forced underground by their own governments. Furthermore, several of these organizations' leaders, including Adolf Hitler and Vladimir Lenin, were imprisoned and treated as martyrs for their ideals. When their separate governments drove them underground, it became exceedingly difficult to determine not just who was distributing the message but also who backed it. Regardless, their underground tactics were successful, and the Nazi party and their "silent majority" acquired control of the German government, while the Bolsheviks' silent majority rebelled and toppled the government, transforming Russia into the Soviet Union.

Regardless of their political beliefs, individuals who resisted the revolutionary parties' ideologies faced similar consequences, including the loss of business, employment, houses, and/or lives. In the United States, the Democratic party in the southern states performed similar tactics to Republicans and Blacks during the reconstruction period[112] [113] [114]. As previously discussed, these early forms of "cancel culture" would later evolve into more sophisticated forms in the twenty-first century. It is difficult for a young American to comprehend the importance of the First Amendment. It is debatable if this is due to a lack of knowledge or a lack of experience in other countries. When I teach pupils History or Civics, I am not surprised at how ignorant they are. Their reactions are usually astonished as a result of previous examples of speech control and the consequences of such examples. Many organizations support this form of suppression because either they are part of the political party in power or they simply do not want to be the next target of accusations. This was a common technique throughout history, as it is today. Yet, many people have become more tribal as a result of today's techniques.

The only difference between history and today that I can think of is that social media has significantly accelerated information. What used to take weeks or months now just takes minutes or days. This information acceleration was a direct outcome of Evergreen University in 2017 and will continue to use the same tactics and beliefs well into the future. Furthermore, if the repression of expression, freedom, and healthy debate continues, those who are canceled will eventually find a way to coalesce, and the clash of ideologies will occur, as it has throughout human civilized cultures, but at a faster pace.

Questions

1. **Reflect on freedom:** It is imperative to understand your individual rights as well as it's limitations of those Rights. It is wrong to say hateful things just for the sake of being hateful, but should a government or corporation intervene in a form of moral policing? Why or why not? Remember, what is the right thing to say or do today, may not be the same tomorrow. And by surrendering those ideas to another entity, you are surrendering your own ability to regulate yourself.

Case Study VIII: "Moral" Policing: Law and Order For The Sake of Feelings and Agendas

"The most brilliant propagandist technique will yield no success unless one fundamental principle is borne in mind constantly - it must confine itself to a few points and repeat them over and over."

– JOSEPH GOEBBELS (NAZI PROPAGANDIST)

[The basic premise of this case study was that in order to have a meaningful conversation about what is morally acceptable and reasonable for society, we must first recognize that morality and ethics are distinct concepts. Because the pendulum swings both ways, moral policing can go astray and endanger people, even those who would advocate for it.]

As described in a previous chapter, morals and ethics fluctuate depending on your culture and individualistic ideas as a result of your social group. It is troubling that in today's society, what was once known as "canceled culture" has evolved into Moral governance or policing. To summarize, morals may not always imply positivity or goodness when it comes to humanistic principles. Here's a striking example of moral principle variances.

> You are exploring an uncharted region of the world. The weather, while hot and muggy, is stunning. The rainforest here is home to rare and exotic creatures. It's annoying to constantly wipe sweat out of your eyes, but you know what

you have to do. A moral obligation compels you to convert the natives of this region to your faith. It is an honor that your leaders have chosen you to carry out this mission. You left your comfortable home to propagate the moral ideas of your people, and the people back home applauded and loved you for it. If you're doing things right, you have no chance of failing. You construct a route through the undergrowth and locate a suitable camping and fortification site. After a long day of setting up camp, you collapse onto the grass for a well-deserved nap. You raise your gaze to the heavens and feel a sense of fulfillment. The initial stage is complete. You close your eyes and find yourself drifting off into a dreamlike state. You've spread your message and your principles have been embraced by strangers, so the dream ends beautifully and you're on your way home, filled with pride. All ears are on you. Many publishers are offering to pay you to write books. The strategy is working, and justice was done. You hear the sound of approaching feet, and as you open your eyes, tribal members are holding spears to your throat. They bind you. Despite your best efforts, they cannot comprehend the appeal you're making to them. They are frightened and confused, but you try to reassure them that you are there to help. You've walked for hours and begged at multiple individuals until you reach a city with enormous temples. They start chanting. It's not only you who's been taken in. When you reach the top of the temple's steep stairs, you'll notice a man decked out in what look to be elaborate masks, feathers, and strange symbols. Undoubtedly, he is the leader. You can't help but wish you understood what he's chanting and shouting about. They're going to tie you up and make you lie down on this bench made of stone. The reason you came back to this place becomes clear to you: to convince these people that your moral viewpoints are legitimate. Almost everything about this is immoral. You start yelling at them to stop, sobbing and screaming, and then you spot the man with the feathers brandishing a knife. Over your head, the man with the feathers brandishes a knife. "No, please!" you say. I've come to..." A tremendous pain suddenly strikes your stomach, you get chilly, everything becomes dark... you wonder was this a dream?

This is a fictional story that is based on the history of the Spanish Missionaries and the Mayan Kingdom. The Mayans were, based on their culture, morally justified in using these strangers as sacrifices, whereas Spanish missionaries were morally justified in forcing Natives to convert. A moral tradition in Maya culture would be human sacrifice for their Gods since blood was seen as a valuable source of food or "life-force" for the Maya deities. It was the correct thing to do in their opinion. This, however, was not "moral policing," but rather a moral precept. This contradicts other morals that may reject human sacrifice. Do you consider it morally acceptable to cut out the intestines of another living human because your God needs it for nourishment? I hope your response is consistent with mine. However, moral conflicts have historically resulted in massive wars, particularly those based on religion. Nonetheless, we are currently witnessing moral battles all across the world. We are entering a new era in which "policing" is focused on moral standards while ignoring the ethics of the means of implementing those moral norms.

Moral policing, like the word itself, has several meanings depending on the source. Yet, the most basic definition is when a group imposes its morals on others who are most likely not members of the same group. This can be based on government regulations, corporate practices, or vigilante organizations. Any of these modes of moral policing can and almost certainly will clash with the morals of other groups or minorities within the oppressing moral majority. As an example, The United States Supreme Court decided in Jacobellis v. Ohio (1964) whether Ohio state could ban Louis Malle's film "The Lovers" because of a "obscene" scene constituted a violation of the First Amendment. This moral contradiction between the freedom of expression guaranteed by the First Amendment and the "obscene" sexual scene. The Supreme Court, the highest court in the United States judicial system, ruled in favor of the picture, claiming that it was constitutionally protected, but what was notable was that the court was unable to articulate their reasoning. With the exception of Chief Justice Earl Warren, the Justices who agreed with the film were divided on why they made their conclusion. However, it was the most famous statement by Associate Justice Potter Stewart that made history: *"I shall not today attempt further to define the kinds of material I understand to be embraced within that shorthand description ["hard-core pornography"], and perhaps I could never succeed in intelligibly doing so. But I know it when I see it, and the motion picture involved in this case is not that."*[15]. This decision was informed by his moral principles and understanding of the law. The same can be said for same-sex marriage, which was prohibited (primarily for moral grounds) until 2015. In other words, from the establishment of the United States and its Constitution in 1789, there have been no federal rights for same-sex couples to marry. Roe v. Wade (410 U.S. 113), decided in 1973, was once interpreted as the United States Constitution protection of women's right to an abortion without undue limitations. Some states have taken it a step further and introduced no term abortion limits which means someone can have an abortion after the third trimester. Depending on who you ask, these problems all involve moral conflicts, and both situations are still debated among traditional Conservatives and Liberals today. Yet, if you believe that such concerns exist just in the United States, you are gravely mistaken. Many countries have significant legal consequences for moral issues. Male homosexuality, for example, is unlawful and penalized in the Middle Eastern countries of Kuwait, Egypt, Oman, and Syria. Furthermore, it is a capital offense in Iran, Saudi Arabia, and the United Arab Emirates. Several other countries have sexuality limits, but regardless of your moral view on the issue, the truth is that it is founded on principles. Moreover, if we reexamine the Mayans' moral beliefs in human sacrifice, we must question ourselves, does your moral worth outweigh the moral values of others? Although these are cultural and legal in character to their separate nations, the same morals may be found within organizations.

Developing moral character in the workforce is a strategy used by businesses to unite their staff and create a culture within. A firm may develop a quarterly or annual tradition that promotes unity through moral ideals (health, political ideologies, lifestyles, etc). The organization may pay their employees for voluntary work if it is on the company's approved list. Of course, prior to volunteering, it must be appropriate and approved within the organization. Finally, matching contributions to non-profit groups supported by the firm is another type of moral solidarity. A record of these gatherings, salaries, and gifts is kept for audit purposes, but who's to say they won't use it for YOUR promotion? I am convinced that most executives will refuse to promote someone who does not suit the company's culture. In other words, in order to succeed, you must adhere to the company's morale ideals. I'm not saying it's bad or right, just expressing an honest opinion. When you are an outspoken green energy advocate, your chances of rising through the ranks of an oil business are little to none. When your moral opinions are prolife and conservatism, the same rules apply to someone working in an organization that promotes pro-choice and progressive ideals. This brings me to the topic of Moral Policing.

Prominent organizations have publicly and financially stated their moral convictions. Employees have been alienated and terminated as a result of not adhering to the organization's moral ideals. This action raises a significant ethical question: do your moral convictions justify destroying someone's financial well-being and future prospects? And, like past missionaries, courts, and governments, many people in positions of power have begun policing moral standards through force or action without the passage of any laws. This can be seen in social media, the news media, and politics. To elaborate, several social media platforms have policies that prohibit hate speech. Yet, hate speech is not always defined. Several supporters of this strategy have different meanings, but they are all difficult to define. In many ways, they define it as "I know it when I see it," as Justice Stewart did. Which brings us to their moral principles. The dangers of basing laws, policies, and rationale only on moral considerations are that they might alter with time, resulting in the opposite end that you desired. As a result, what is "correct" now may be "wrong" tomorrow. The news media generates a lot more money off of emotions, and nothing brings people together more emotionally than common moral ideals being broken. During the 2020 protests and riots, numerous news outlets employed rhetoric to not only promote their moral beliefs but also to attack those who disagreed with them.

In politics, the same can be said. Like the Catholic Crusades of the 11th century, which were pushed by Pope Urban II, who believed that killing non-Christians is not a sin and that capturing the Holy Land guarantees forgiveness for all your sins, if you push your moral beliefs to others, you are not only right but justified. Throughout their debates, members of Congress and those competing for the democratic ticket for President in 2020 used moral themes. Several people utilize various types of rhetoric to demonstrate how their moral theory was not only logical but also ethical. Some encouraged the riots and bloodshed to continue as a moral obligation. They, like Pope Urban II, gave an excuse for those with similar moral ideals to attack others and do nearly $1.4 billion in damage as of this writing[116]. For many insurance companies, this will result in increased premiums for all other insurance holders when many people cannot afford the existing cost of insurance. This trickle effect is not unusual, and historians believe the crusades were the impetus for the Middle Eastern wars. Nevertheless, when political leaders like Representative Maxine Waters encourage people that are in President Trump's cabinet to create a crowd and harass them, one must question their moral principles[117]. It is convenient, like Pope Urban II, when it is up against an opposing foe and may reap the benefits without running the risk of the crowd assaulting a fellow citizen. Do Rep. Maxine Water's moral beliefs take precedence over those of individuals who work closely with the President?

Society as a whole must decide how laws are formed and, more crucially, how they are enforced. The United States was founded on the moral principles of accepting people from various origins. Although slavery was not abolished until 100 years after its start, emancipated Black People led prosperous lives. Yet, when moral values contravene other American liberties, citizens have the legal right to speak out against it. Yet, humans govern America, and all humans have problems. This raises the questions on moral policing as a whole. That is in our history, and yet we continue to make the same mistakes. Many people agree with the mistakes of moral traditions based on moral disparities, such as human sacrifice, forced religious conversion, and massacre's, but are prepared to look away when their moral beliefs are "better" because they feel justified. In effect, they become oppressors. When a mass of people forces pedestrians and observers to hand signal allegiances or face harassment and judgment, the fact remains the same. Their moral superiority becomes no different than that of the Mayan empire's Spanish missionaries.

Questions

1. **Reflect on Moral Policing:** How can one make sure laws are fair to all people that have different morals and yet still be ethical?
   - **NOTE:** This is a question that lawmakers have struggled with for many years. In essence, there is no real right or wrong answer because your morals principles may creep in directly or indirectly.
2. **Question:** Describe in your own words when moral principles are justified over other people's values.
3. **Small Project-Based Practice:** Create a venn diagram of a moral issue in your community. Find common beliefs as well as differences. Once analyzed, determine if you are being biased towards one particular belief over another. This can easily be identified when you find more sources of one over another. You need to challenge yourself to find at least equal to the amount of reasons for something you don't agree with. Also, keep the quality high. Simply finding simple reasons or deciding there are no justification is lazy at best, malicious at worst.

PART TEN

Conclusion and Next Steps

XXI

Chapter 21: Develop "Thick Skin": Criticism is Part of The Process, Not The Result.

"If someone is able to show me that what I think or do is not right, I will happily change, for I seek the truth, by which no one was ever truly harmed. It is the person who continues in his self-deception and ignorance who is harmed."

—MARCUS AURELIUS

Being a self-corrective thinker is one of the most difficult aspects of a critical thinker. It takes humility and the ability to admit to everyone, including yourself, that you were incorrect about this decision, judgment, or conviction. Furthermore, because of social media and on-line "anonymous" bullying, the potential of being ridiculed for being mistaken in the twenty-first century is significant. In other words, you must get thick skin. Yet, for the majority of individuals, it is not as simple as it appears, and it takes courage and inner fortitude to accept criticism after a self-corrective moment. Some of the most confident persons I have met in my life and those that are either very stubborn and set in their ways or the sharpest critical thinkers are veterans in the armed forces. Not just any veteran, mind you, but combat special operations veterans. Let us first examine the fact that everybody who joins the military must be broken down and rebuilt in order to fit to a doctrine or culture. This needs developing self-confidence in order to achieve goals that may appear near-impossible at first. To be a part of a special operations unit, an elite class of soldiers that is significantly less populated than the military community as a whole, a selection process that is designed to select individuals who can not only withstand high levels of stress but can also make proper critical thinking decisions, is now required. Many military people can handle the "fight or flight response" as an involuntary physiological reaction, but doing so while applying critical thinking elevates warfare to a new level. The selection procedure for Special Operation operators requires a critical thinker who can study a situation, make a decision, and act on that decision under extreme stress. This decision can mean the difference between life and death for themselves, or, in the worst-case scenario, for their fellow operators and the people they are attempting to protect. This needs self-confidence in your capacity to make judgments based on the information you have at the time, as well as your ability to execute on those decisions.

There are few jobs in the world with such high stakes. The US military, in particular, has been conducting ongoing research on this topic, analyzing decision making and the outcomes through doctrines and studies such as the "Military Decision-Making" process, which requires you to not only understand the mission, but also produce an OPORD (or operation order) using proper judgment, logic, and planning to make a decision and act on that decision. Furthermore, the commander may finish their orders and battle rehearsals only to receive a FRAGO (or fragmentation order) requiring them to change their initial strategy. What is equally crucial, and sometimes overlooked, is the debriefing following the mission. For the special operators, it is not only about what may be revealed to the public and what must remain classified, but also about what went well and what went wrong. They examine their decisions and learn from their mistakes as well as what might be improved. This is crucial not only for operators, but for critical thinkers in general. Self-corrective thinking includes not only what decisions or judgments you made incorrectly, but also what could be improved from the correct decisions.

Doctors must follow the same procedure. A physician must utilize self-corrective thinking to heal a patient if they misdiagnosed them, whether through overprescribing medication or miscalculating the condition. Fellow physicians may provide advice or appropriate treatment to the other doctor's patient. This is both a learning experience for the doctor and a benefit to the patient. Accepting correction and criticism requires a large amount of self-confidence.

Here is when humility comes into play. There are various methods for developing what I call thick skin. You must instill confidence in yourself in any way you can. Exercising has been my personal "go to" for confidence building. Doing it not only boosts your confidence, but it also raises endorphins, dopamine, serotonin, and norepinephrine, all of which are involved in controlling your mood and brain chemistry[118]. Furthermore, being able to look in the mirror and feel confident in yourself is a vital attribute to possess. Unfortunately, this is not the end of the story. You must discover an outlet that makes you happy. This could be reading, writing, playing video games, or listening to music. You need an outlet in particular when you are heartbroken by a decision or judgment in which you have emotionally involved and which you later discover to be incorrect. Furthermore, this outlet should be limited to only you and no one else. This is done to avoid issues if, and only if, the bad decision concerns that specific person. However, your confidence must be your own and not based on the opinions of others.

Although confidence might assist you in overcoming some of the emotions associated with self-corrective thinking, it is not the be-all and end-all. There may come a moment when someone tries to "correct" you who is not actually correct and is just trying to get under your skin with their arguments. There may also be some who have no self-correction skills and are set in their ways. They lack critical thinking skills. The first thing you should do is assess the other party's intentions. You can't help people who only wish to hurt you, and you shouldn't feel obligated to change the views of those who can't be corrected due to hubris. Many fights or arguments with these people are meaningless. Sometimes it's best to simply say "agree to disagree" and walk away, or to call them out on their indecency and go away. Whatever decision you pick, you always leave the argument. It is critical to understand that stupid people cannot be reasoned with. If you must confront it, approach the individual and do not be scared to walk away. There is sufficient historical evidence from many wise people as well as a range of religious books to show that this is the wisest course of action. There will always be people with whom you cannot argue, and that is perfectly fine. You are involved in self-corrective thinking. It is your responsibility to correct your original decision when you discover something new. Don't let fools and idiots turn you into one.

Having thick skin means not taking things personally. Furthermore, it is about elevating self-corrective thinking to a logical level rather than an emotional one. We are not flawless, but we may use these tactics to manage our behaviors, judgments, decisions, and reactions. Just like the special operators in the armed services and the physicians who attend to their patients, it is necessary to be a self-corrective thinker with thick skin. Accept that you do not know everything and that this is just fine! When we lose our ability to learn from faulty decisions, judgments, and beliefs, we lose sight of what it is to be a critical thinker. Furthermore, you must be able to "debrief" your activities and identify strategies to improve future outcomes. This will help you grow not only as a critical thinker, but also as a person.

Questions

1. List some decisions you have made that ended well. Why did it end well? Elaborate and break down each step you took to conclude that decision.
   ◦ Was there anything you could have done better from that decision?
2. List some decisions you have made that ended poorly. Why did it not end well? Elaborate and break down each step you took to conclude that decision.
   ◦ Was there anything you could have done for a better outcome?

XXII

Chapter 22: The Importance of Critical Thinking in Shaping Our Personal and Professional Lives

"Logical thinking keeps you from wasting time worrying, or hoping. It prevents disappointment. Imagination, on the other hand, only gets you hyped up over things that will never realistically happen."

—JODI PICOULT

Within the pages of this book, we have investigated the fundamental concepts of critical thinking as well as its practical applications in a variety of spheres of life, including personal relationships, the workplace, debates, and case studies. We have talked about how critical thinking gives us the ability to evaluate arguments, get over cognitive biases, and arrive at well-informed conclusions based on evidence and reasoning.

The idea that critical thinking is a skill that can be learned and improved with practice is one of the most important things that may be gained from reading this book. It is not a talent that some people are born with and others are not; everyone has the same opportunity to develop it. By developing a grasp of the process of critical thinking and engaging in frequent practice with it, we can enhance our capacity to examine and evaluate arguments, steer clear of common logical fallacies, and come to more sound conclusions.

critical thinking is not merely a talent possessed by academics or working professionals; rather, it is a vital life skill from which everyone may significantly benefit. Critical thinking enables us to sort through information, differentiate between facts and views, and make sense of complicated problems regardless of whether we are making decisions about our own lives, reading the news, or participating in public dialogue.

In addition, critical thinking is becoming an increasingly important skill in the workplace. Employees in today's modern businesses are expected to make rational decisions based on relevant data and evidence, communicate effectively with their coworkers and clients, and be able to adapt to new circumstances and challenges. Employees that can think critically and creatively, solve challenges, and make educated decisions that benefit the organization and its stakeholders are in high demand among employers.

It is crucial for democracy because it enables voters to assess the arguments and evidence offered by politicians and to make educated decisions based on their own values and views. This makes critical thinking an essential component of democracy. Critical thinking is a powerful technique that can be used to navigate the complicated and often perplexing environment of modern politics. In a world when misinformation, propaganda, and fake news are commonplace, this is especially important.

The significance of critical thinking goes well beyond our individual and professional spheres of existence; it is an indispensable instrument for influencing the course of both the future of our society and the future of the entire globe. We can better comprehend the challenges we face and find solutions that are beneficial to everyone if we use critical thinking to issues such as political ideals, inequality, and in local communities.

The ability to think in a rational manner is absolutely necessary for navigating the intricacies of today's environment. By cultivating and honing our critical thinking skills through regular practice, we may improve the quality of the decisions we make, steer clear of frequent logical errors, and help make our society a better place. Remember the fundamental ideas that we covered in this book and think about how you may implement them in both your personal and professional life as you continue on your own journey of developing critical thinking. You will be able to accomplish your goals, find solutions to issues, and have a beneficial effect on the world if you have the logical mind.

Questions

1. Now that you have completed the book, name 10 takeaways from the book. Why did they stand out?
2. What can you do to continue to develop your logical mind?

Next Steps

Thank you for reading:

THE LOGICAL MIND

Learn Critical Thinking to Make Better Choices

For additional free content, more information on upcoming courses/books, future updates, and the author newsletters, please register at:

www.MAAponte.com

The *Thinking 2 Think* podcast is hosted by the author and is available on your preferred podcast app:

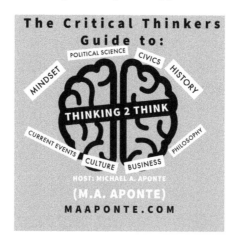

Endnotes

1. Edwin A. Locke, Toward a theory of task motivation and incentives, Organizational Behavior and Human Performance, Volume 3, Issue 2, 1968, Pages 157-189

2. Doran, G. T. (1981). There's a S.M.A.R.T. Way to Write Management's Goals and Objectives. Management Review, 70, 35-36.

3. Lenin, What Is To Be Done?, "The Plan For an All-Russia Political Newspaper" (1901) https://www.marxists.org/archive/lenin/quotes.htm

4. Little, Becky, When Cigarette Companies Used Doctors to Push Smoking (2019), https://www.history.com/news/cigarette-ads-doctors-smoking-endorsement

5. King, Gilbert. "The Silence that Preceded China's Great Leap into Famine". Smithsonian. Retrieved November 28, 2019.

6. Durdin, Tillman (May 19, 1971), "China Transformed By Elimination of 'Four Olds.'". New York Times, P. 14

7. Johnson, I. (2020, July 10). Who Killed More: Hitler, Stalin, or Mao? | Ian Johnson | The New York Review of Books. The New York Review of Books. https://www.nybooks.com/daily/2018/02/05/who-killed-more-hitler-stalin-or-mao/

8. Steinbuch, Yaron (June 25, 2020). Black Lives Matter co-founder describes herself as 'trained Marxist', New York Post

9. Marx, Karl (1891). "Critique of the Gotha Programme".

10. Karl Marx & Friedrich Engels (1848), Manifesto of the Communist Party.

11. Del Rosario-Tapan, C. (2022, September 13). In Solidarity. We raise our voices. Thousand Currents. https://thousandcurrents.org/black-lives-matter/

12. Harrell, Erika, Ph.D., Black Victims of Violent Crime (2007), Bureau of Justice Statistics, https://www.bjs.gov/content/pub/pdf/bvvc.pdf

13. Lenin, V. (n.d.). Lenin: Two Tactics of Social-Democracy in the Democratic Revolution. https://www.marxists.org/archive/lenin/works/1905/tactics/index.htm

14. Eddy, Paul; Boyd, Gregory (2007). The Jesus Legend: A Case for the Historical Reliability of the Synoptic Jesus Tradition, Baker Academic, ISBN 0-8010-3114-1

15. Muhammad Qasim Zaman (1997). Religion and Politics Under the Early 'abbāsids: The Emergence of the Proto-Sunnī Elite (Islamic History and Civilization). ISBN 978-90-04-10678-9.

16. Maslow, A.H. (1943). "A theory of human motivation". Psychological Review.

17. Ankel, S. (2020, July 18). National Museum of African American History apologizes for chart listing attributes of "whiteness" after criticism from Donald Trump Jr and the conservative media. Insider. https://www.insider.com/african-american-museum-in-dc-apologizes-for-whiteness-chart-2020-7

18. Emiko Ohnuki-Tierney (29 June 1984). Illness and Culture in Contemporary Japan: An Anthropological View. Cambridge University Press. p. 67. ISBN 978-0-521-27786-0.

19. Cleary, T. F. (2008). Training the samurai mind: A bushido sourcebook. Shambhala.

20. Inazo Nitobe (1905, Copyright 2013), Code of the Samurai Bushido: The Soul of Japan, Amber Books Ltd.London, UK.

21. Meiji Restoration, https://www.history.com/topics/japan/meiji-restoration

22. Dmitri Volkogonov (1995), Lenin: Life and Legacy

23. Nell, William (1855). The Colored Patriots of the American Revolution

24. Marx, Karl (1891). "Critique of the Gotha Programme".

25. Werth, Nicolas & Paczkowski, Andrzej (1999), The Black Book of Communism, Harvard University Press

26. "Marxists Internet Archive": https://www.marxists.org/glossary/terms/i/n.htm

27. López León, Dorian. "Puerto Rico in the 16th century – History". Encyclopedia de Puerto Rico. Puerto Rico Endowment for the Humanities, and the National Endowment for the Humanities

28. Robert Wright, Richard (1941). "Negro Companions of the Spanish Explorers". Phylon. 2 (4).

29. Hiebert, F., Altoff, P., & Fischer, F. (2018), U.S. History: American Stories Beginnings to 1877. Chicago, IL. National Geographic Learning | Cengage

30. Times, N. Y. (2021, November 9). The 1619 Project. The New York Times. https://www.nytimes.com/interactive/2019/08/14/magazine/1619-america-slavery.html

31. Tetlow, Elisabeth Meier (2004). "Sumer". Women, Crime and Punishment in Ancient Law and Society: Volume 1: The Ancient Near East. Women, Crime, and Punishment in Ancient Law and Society. 1. New York: A&C Black. p. 7. ISBN 9780826416285.

32. Campbell, Gwyn. The Structure of Slavery in Indian Ocean Africa and Asia (Frank Cass, 2004)

33. Davis, Robert C., Christian Slaves, Muslim Masters: White Slavery in the Mediterranean, The Barbary Coast, and Italy, 1500–1800 (Palgrave Macmillan, New York, 2003) ISBN 0333719662

34. Blakemore, Erin, How an Enslaved African Man in Boston Helped Save Generations from Smallpox, History.com, https://www.history.com/news/smallpox-vaccine-onesimus-slave-cotton-mather

35. Phillis Wheatley. (2023, March 7). Biography. https://www.biography.com/writer/phillis-wheatley

36. Mark Jarrett & Robert Yahng (2017), Gateway to Early American History 2nd Edition. Lafayette, CA. Florida Transformative Education

37. Salsa - History of the Salsa Dance. (n.d.). http://www.dancefacts.net/dance-history/history-of-salsa/

38. James Armistead Lafayette. (n.d.). American Battlefield Trust. https://www.battlefields.org/learn/biographies/james-armistead-lafayette

39. What is Modern Slavery? - United States Department of State. (2020, December 1). United States Department of State. https://www.state.gov/what-is-modern-slavery/

40. Karl Marx & Friedrich Engels (1848), Manifesto of the Communist Party.

41. Dmitri Volkogonov (1995), Lenin: Life and Legacy

42. Little, Becky, How Woodrow Wilson Tried to Reverse Black American Progress (2020), https://www.history.com/news/woodrow-wilson-racial-segregation-jim-crow-ku-klux-klan

43. Cooper, J. M. (2023, January 30). Woodrow Wilson | Biography, Presidency, & Accomplishments. Encyclopedia Britannica. https://www.britannica.com/biography/Woodrow-Wilson

44. Philip Van Doren Stern (1940), The Life And Writings of Abraham Lincoln. Toronto, Canada. Random House, Inc.

45. Castel, Albert E. (1979). American Presidency. Lawrence, Kan.: The Regents Press of Kansas. ISBN 978-0-7006-0190-5.

46. Hiebert, F., Altoff, P., & Fischer, F. (2018), U.S. History: American Stories Beginnings to 1877. Chicago, IL. National Geographic Learning | Cengage

47. Little, Becky, How Woodrow Wilson Tried to Reverse Black American Progress (2020), https://www.history.com/news/woodrow-wilson-racial-segregation-jim-crow-ku-klux-klan

48. Wilder, Craig Steven (2005). In The Company Of Black Men: The African Influence on African American. NYU Press. ISBN 9780814793695.

49. Nell, William (1855). The Colored Patriots of the American Revolution

50. Naval History Magazine. (2019, September 20). U.S. Naval Institute. https://www.navalhistory.org/2019/09/20/hispanic-heritage-month-david-glasgow-farragut

51. Little, Becky, How Woodrow Wilson Tried to Reverse Black American Progress (2020), https://www.history.com/news/woodrow-wilson-racial-segregation-jim-crow-ku-klux-klan

52. Woodrow Wilson | Biography, Presidency, & Accomplishments. (2023, January 30). Encyclopedia Britannica. https://www.britannica.com/biography/Woodrow-Wilson/Second-term-as-president

53. Book Burning. (n.d.). https://encyclopedia.ushmm.org/content/en/article/book-burning

54. Stelmakh, V. D. "Reading in the Context of Censorship in the Soviet Union",

Libraries & Culture - Volume 36, Number 1, Winter 2001, pp. 143–151, University of Texas Press

55. Definition of socialism. (2023). In Merriam-Webster Dictionary. https://www.merriam-webster.com/dictionary/socialism

56. "World: Europe US banks gave Jewish money to Nazis". BBC News. BBC. February 3, 1999.

57. "World: Europe US banks gave Jewish money to Nazis". BBC News. BBC. February 3, 1999.

58. Bukharin, Nikolai (1920). The ABC of Communism. Penguin Books, 1969

59. "IAF principles". International of Anarchist Federations. Archived from the original on 5 January 2012. The IAF – IFA fights for : the abolition of all forms of authority whether economical, political, social, religious, cultural or sexual. https://web.archive.org/web/20120105095946/http://www.iaf-ifa.org/principles/english.html

60. Slevin, Carl. "Anarchism." The Concise Oxford Dictionary of Politics. Ed. Iain McLean and Alistair McMillan. Oxford University Press, 2003.

61. James, Ian (4 October 2012). "Venezuela vote puts 'Chavismo' to critical test". Yahoo. Archived from the original on 5 December 2014.

62. Charlie Devereux & Raymond Colitt. 7 March 2013. "Venezuelans' Quality of Life Improved in UN Index Under Chavez". Bloomberg L.P. Archived from the original on 7 November 2014

63. Cristóbal Nagel, Juan (4 June 2014). "Poverty Shoots Up in Venezuela". Foreign Policy. https://foreignpolicy.com/2014/06/04/poverty-shoots-up-in-venezuela/

64. de Córdoba, José; Vyas, Kejal (9 December 2012). "Venezuela's Future in Balance". The Wall Street Journal.

65. The Editors of Encyclopaedia Britannica. (1998, July 20). Nazi Party | Definition, Meaning, History, & Facts. Encyclopedia Britannica. https://www.britannica.com/topic/Nazi-Party

66. Ray, M. (n.d.). Were the Nazis Socialists? Encyclopedia Britannica. https://www.britannica.com/story/were-the-nazis-socialists

67. "Nestlé paid $14.6 million for using slave labor". The Independent. 2000-08-28. Archived from the original on 2015-07-03.

68. Moskowitz, Sanford L. (2009). "Bayer". In Charles Wankel (ed.). Encyclopedia of Business in Today's World. SAGE Publications. pp. 126–128.

69. "World: Europe US banks gave Jewish money to Nazis". BBC News. BBC. February 3, 1999.

70. Schmid, John; Tribune, International Herald (1999-02-05). "Deutsche Bank Linked To Auschwitz Funding". The New York Times. ISSN 0362-4331.

71. Eadon, Glen; Hawkins, John (June 1, 2008). The Nazi Hydra in America: Suppressed History of a Century. Joshua Tree, California: Progressive Press. p. 195. ISBN 9780930852436.

72. Edwin Black (2001). IBM and the Holocaust: The Strategic Alliance Between Nazi Germany and America's Most Powerful Corporation. ISBN 0-316-85769-6.

73. Kay, Anthony (2002). German Jet Engine and Gas Turbine Development 1930-1945. Airlife Publishing. ISBN 9781840372946.

74. Köster, Roman. "Hugo Boss, 1924-1945. A Clothing Factory During the Weimar Republic and Third Reich" https://web.archive.org/web/20111108165733/http://group.hugoboss.com/files/Study_on_the_Companys_History_Abridged_Verson_en_final.pdf

75. "German industry unveils Holocaust fund". BBC News. 1999-02-16 http://news.bbc.co.uk/2/hi/business/280475.stm

76. Rusian Revolution (2022), History.com, https://www.history.com/topics/russia/russian-revolution

77. Dmitri Volkogonov (1995), Lenin: Life and Legacy

78. Wydra, Harald (September 2012). "The Power of Symbols—Communism and Beyond". International Journal of Politics, Culture, and Society. 25 (1–3): 49–69. doi:10.1007/s10767-011-9116-x. ISSN 0891-4486.

79. Riasanovsky, Nichlas V.; Steinberg, Mark D. (2005). A History of Russia (7th ed.). Oxford University Press. ISBN 978-0195153941.

80. Robert Service. Stalin: A Biography. 2004. ISBN 978-0-330-41913-0

81. Aleksandr I. Solzhenitsyn (1973). The Gulag Archipelago. Harper & Row

82. Werth, Nicolas & Paczkowski, Andrzej (1999), The Black Book of Communism, Harvard University Press

83. Riasanovsky, Nichlas V.; Steinberg, Mark D. (2005). A History of Russia (7th ed.). Oxford University Press. ISBN 978-0195153941.

84. Norbert Francis, "Revolution in Russia and China: 100 Years," 6 (July 2017): 130-143.

85. O'Hara, Phillip (March 19, 1999). *Encyclopedia of Political Economy: L-Z.* Routledge. p. 1248. ISBN 978-0415154260

86. Munger, M. (2021, March 17). Capitalism Saved Sweden. AIER. https://www.aier.org/article/capitalism-saved-sweden/

87. Index of Economic Freedom: Promoting Economic Opportunity and Prosperity by Country. (n.d.). Index of Ecnmic Freedom. https://www.heritage.org/index/

88. Index of Economic Freedom: Promoting Economic Opportunity and Prosperity by Country. (n.d.). Index of Ecnmic Freedom. https://www.heritage.org/index/

89. Bick, J. (2005, May 29). The Microsoft Millionaires Come of Age. The New York Times. https://www.nytimes.com/2005/05/29/business/yourmoney/the-microsoft-millionaires-come-of-age.html

90. Solzhenitsyn, Aleksandr (1973). *The Gulag Archipelago* (English ed. 1974). Éditions du Seuil, France

91. Taleb, Nassim Nicholas (2018), *Skin in the Game: Hidden Asymmetries in Daily Life*, Random House

92. Boston Massacre, https://www.history.com/topics/american-revolution/boston-massacre

93. Crispus Attucks. (2023, March 7). Biography. https://www.biography.com/military-figure/crispus-attucks

94. Pruitt, Sarah, Jefferson & Adams: Founding Frenemies (r2020, 2016), https://www.history.com/news/jefferson-adams-founding-frenemies

95. What Type of Speech Is Not Protected by the First Amendment?, https://www.hg.org/legal-articles/what-type-of-speech-is-not-protected-by-the-first-amendment-34258

96. Markman, A., PhD. (2019, October 2). What Does Advertising Do? Psychology Today. https://www.psychologytoday.com/us/blog/ulterior-motives/201008/what-does-advertising-do

97. NYC Mayor de Blasio says protests are largely peaceful, curfew will continue. (2020, June 5). PBS NewsHour. https://www.pbs.org/newshour/nation/watch-nyc-mayor-de-blasio-says-protests-are-largely-peaceful-curfew-will-continue

98. Diano, M., Celeghin, A., Bagnis, A., & Tamietto, M. (2017). Amygdala Response to Emotional Stimuli without Awareness: Facts and Interpretations. Frontiers in Psychology, 7. https://doi.org/10.3389/fpsyg.2016.02029

99. Existing Organizations | Stay Exempt. (n.d.). https://www.stayexempt.irs.gov/home/existing-organizations/existing-organizations

100. Fritz, J. (2020, September 17). How the IRS Classifies Nonprofit Organizations. LiveAbout. https://www.thebalancesmb.com/how-the-irs-classifies-nonprofit-organizations-2501798

101. Definition of fake news. (n.d.). In www.dictionary.com. https://www.dictionary.com/browse/fake-news

102. Definition of propaganda. (n.d.). In www.dictionary.com. https://www.dictionary.com/browse/propaganda

103. History.com Editors. (2022, November 30). Black History Month. HISTORY. https://www.history.com/topics/black-history/black-history-month

104. Blakemore, E. (2020, June 19). The Revolutionary War Hero Who Was Openly Gay. HISTORY. https://www.history.com/news/openly-gay-revolutionary-war-hero-friedrich-von-steuben

105. Industrial Revolution and the Standard of Living - Econlib. (2018, June 27). Econlib. https://www.econlib.org/library/Enc/IndustrialRevolutionandtheStandardofLiving.html

106. Ackerman, Kenneth D., Young J. Edgar: Hoover, the Red Scare, and the Assault on Civil Liberties (NY: Carroll & Graf, 2007)

107. Loftus, Geoff. (2009). "Introduction to Psychology (15th Ed.)".- Chapter 3

108. Mounk, Y. (2018, October 10). What the New Sokal Hoax Reveals About Academia. The Atlantic. https://www.theatlantic.com/ideas/archive/2018/10/new-sokal-hoax/572212/

109. Borschel-Dan, A. (2018, October 5). Duped academic journal

publishes rewrite of 'Mein Kampf' as feminist manifesto. Times of Israel. https://www.timesofisrael.com/duped-academic-journal-publishes-rewrite-of-mein-kampf-as-feminist-manifesto/

110. National Archives |. (n.d.). https://www.archives.gov/

111. Cato Poll: 62% of Americans Say They Have Political Views They're Afraid to Share; https://www.cato.org/publications/survey-reports/poll-62-americans-say-they-have-political-views-theyre-afraid-share#50-strong-liberals-support-firing-trump-donors-36-strong-conservatives-support-firing-biden-donors

112. Reconstruction, History.com, https://www.history.com/topics/american-civil-war/reconstruction

113. McDonough, Frank (2003). *Hitler and the Rise of the Nazi Party.* Pearson/Longman. ISBN 978-0582506060.

114. Dmitri Volkogonov (1995), Lenin: Life and Legacy

115. 378 U.S. at 197 (Stewart, J., Concuring)

116. Insurance Information Institute; https://www.iii.org/fact-statistic/facts-statistics-civil-disorders

117. Ehrlich, Jamie, (2018), *Maxine Waters encourages supporters to harass Trump administration officials,* CNN https://www.cnn.com/2018/06/25/politics/maxine-waters-trump-officials/index.html

118. Dfarhud D, Malmir M, Khanahmadi M. Happiness & Health: The Biological Factors- Systematic Review Article. Iran J Public Health. 2014 Nov;43(11):1468-77. PMID: 26060713; PMCID: PMC4449495.

119. Morrison, A. (2023, May 26). New Black Lives Matter tax documents show foundation is tightening its belt, has $30M in assets | AP News. AP News. https://apnews.com/article/black-lives-matter-donations-george-floyd-protests-ddcfod21d130a5d46256aa6c5d145ea7

120. The Greatest Lie Ever Sold (2022). The Daily Wire. https://www.dailywire.com/videos/the-greatest-lie-ever-sold

121. Kerr, A. (2022, February 4). Washington Examiner. Washington Examiner. https://www.washingtonexaminer.com/news/blms-millions-go-unaccounted-for-after-leaders-quietly-jump-ship

Michael Antonio Aponte (M.A. Aponte) is an accomplished author, motivational speaker, and educator who is committed to empowering people through critical thinking. M.A. Aponte has made a significant impact in a variety of fields due to his diverse background and extensive experience. He began his career at Merrill Lynch as a wealth manager, where he gained valuable insights into finance and its impact on our lives. His knowledge in this field has assisted many people in making sound financial decisions. Later, he transitioned into the role of motivational speaker on his journey of personal and professional growth, inspiring and mentoring people from all walks of life. He has shared his wisdom and inspired others to reach their full potential through his speeches and guidance.

M.A. Aponte also worked as a field training officer for the New York City Police Department, where he honed his leadership abilities and gained a comprehensive understanding of human behavior and societal dynamics. He later pursued a career in the social sciences as an educator because of his interest in education and philosophy. He has dedicated himself to teaching others how to approach life's challenges with a discerning and thoughtful mindset, with a focus on critical thinking.

M.A. Aponte has written insightful essays on a variety of topics, including current events, finance, history, and philosophy, based on his knowledge and experience. His writings reflect his intellectual curiosity and dedication to investigating ideas that shape our world. He continues to share his expertise, insights, and perspectives through his works, motivated by a genuine desire to empower others. You will be inspired by his words to question, analyze, and embrace the power of a logical mind, ultimately gaining new perspectives that can shape a brighter future.

The Thinking 2 Think podcast is hosted by the author and is available on your preferred podcast app: https://thinking2think.buzzsprout.com